Praises for
THE BOUTIQUE BIBLE

Two decades is a major accomplishment, especially from a partnership consisting of women. The world always says that women can't work together. This book proves that wrong.

Nelly Bernal,
Women's Shoe Designer

I appreciated the honesty that The Boutique Bible allowed to shine through. So many entrepreneurs pretend that every day is good. This book proves that there will be cloudy days but in the end, hard work pays off.

Lady Jade,
Nationally Syndicated Morning Radio Co-Host

This book was filled with far more than what I could have imagined. From real stories and testaments to insightful ways to put my thoughts into action and even a place to journal. Powerful!

Ashley Antoinette,
NY Times Bestselling Author

The Boutique Bible was a play on innovation from beginning to end and showed the rise to success that many fail to speak on.

Latoya Logan, CEO & Founder of Latoya
Logan Hair Collection

An honest story of a will to win and the unmatched determination of women on a mission to pursue their dreams.

Catrina Brown,
Founder & CEO of House of Tinks

The Boutique BIBLE

THOU SHALL SECURE THINE OWN BAG

Tiffanie Mims &
Alexis Weekley

The Boutique Bible books may be purchased for educational, business or promotional use. For information, please email the Sales Department at info@bdonnasbosses.com

Printed in the U.S.A.
First Printing, January 2020

Library of Congress Cataloging-in-Publication Data has been applied for.

ISBN: 978-1-7342346-3-3 (IngramSpark Edition)
ISBN: 979-8-6033230-5-3 (KDP Print)

Dedication

**We dedicate this book to the
future bosses of the world.**

-Tiff & Lex-

And then one day

she built an *empire*

with all of the

bricks that life had

thrown her way.

-Tiff & Lex-

Table of
CONTENTS

Acknowledgements
FROM TIFFANIE

I want to take a minute to sincerely extend a humongous thank you to my family and friends. To my husband Brandon, you've been my Rock. A constant, unwavering, unmoving force. Thank you for having my back, love you so much. To my Sonshine Eury James, a.k.a Eu-Eu...you're my entire world! God truly blessed me when he picked me to be your mother. You're my greatest gift...I'll give everything in me to see you win. To my Mom Vanessa and Grandma Sara, thank you for loving me and raising me. I get my work ethic from you both; I got a chance to see firsthand what hard work looks like and what a strong woman looks like. I love you, Mom & Grandma! To my Brother Anthony, my Aunt Carla, and Aunt Whitney...love you all so much. To the Timms family, Teresa and Mike, you've been a godsend with helping me with Eury since he was a baby. God provided us both an extended family when he led me to you 11 years ago. I can't thank you enough for the love and support.. love you guys!

To FAMU...yep, I'm thanking my Alma Mater Florida A&M University for Hustling Me Up. I know for a fact that without my college experience at FAMU, I wouldn't be here. This school and the city of Tallahassee shaped and molded me into the businesswoman I am today. There would be no Bdonnas without FAMU. #RATTLERNATION

To my Ride or Die, Bdonnas creative director Latrise Sheriff. From the very first day I met you, we forged an organic friendship. From friendship we became family. You've been right there helping Bdonnas reach new heights. Your creativity is unmatched. Your heart is made of pure gold. Bdonnas needed you and you've been here unwavering. I love you!

To my creative team, all of our models and Bdonnas Associates past & present, thank you for sharing your time and talent with us throughout the years. To our photographer D.Lacy, you've been an intricate piece of our success because you've been taking our pictures for the website since day 1. Every single week! We fight like cats & dogs but we appreciate you for putting up with our foolishness LOL. #BdonnasWednesday

Lord only knows where I would be without my girl tribe. Sisterhood means everything to me and my girlfriends light my soul on fire. They are my happy place. I want to thank you all for supporting me and loving on me. My Blues Artisha, Chakita, Telebah, Tia, some of the craziest heffas I've ever met...wouldn't trade them for nothing in the world! Alexis, Jacque, & Latrise my Texas Crew...Thank you for being symbols of togetherness, I love y'all so much. Ersula, we go back since FAMU...your sister-ship has been solid as a rock..love you, sis! To my Day 2 Ashley Antoinette, our friendship came out of nowhere and it's been a divine intervention...you've been such a blessing to my life and I appreciate you so much! Your invaluable wisdom and support of this book project has been unwavering. I'm not even sure if I could repay you for it but knowing you....you would never let me lol. I love you Ash! #AshArmy4Life

Last but certainly not least, to every customer that has ever rocked a BellaDonna Shoes or a Bdonnas piece..WE APPRE-CIATE YOU!! Can't even believe y'all been rocking with us for 20 YEARS! Let's see if we can we rock out 20 more!

Tiffanie

Acknowledgements
FROM ALEXIS

I have to take this moment to say thank you Mommy & Daddy from the bottom of my heart! Mom, as the grammar police, you taught me how to articulate every word correctly and forced me to elevate my writing skills. More importantly, you allowed me to step into my independence early on at 15 years old when I started driving myself & Marques to school every day.

Dad, you immersed us in college campus life during your unforgettable vice presidency at JCSU. I was always so proud that my dad held such a prestigious position at an HBCU. As kids, you gave us a life rich in the black college experience as we attended countless HBCU football games, basketball games, homecomings, Greek step shows, and graduations.

I can't thank you both enough- you never questioned my decisions; instead you co-parented and supported my every move ever since I can remember. I never asked for much, but when I needed money to finance my dreams, y'all did what y'all had to do to make that happen for me, and for that, I am eternally grateful.

God blessed me to have a second mom and a second dad who stood by your sides and also supported me unconditionally. I want to express thanks to my awesome step-mom, Jeannette, and amazing step-dad, Ken.

Special thanks to all of my family for your unwavering love and support. There are far too many of you Robinsons, Tylers, and Bullards for me to name individually, but thanks to my younger brother, Marques Robinson, my niece, Vivian Rolle, and amazing friend, Ebony Coleman. Y'all help hold BellaDonna down and I love you more than you could ever mentally conceive.

To every customer who has ever shopped with BellaDonna Shoes and on bdonnas.com, our success is because of you. Thank you so very much.

To our one and only creative director, Latrise, your talent is priceless. I wish I had an ounce of your magic. Bdonnas.com would not be half of what it is today without you. I knew we needed you on our team from the very first time I saw your Wardrobe On Heels projects. You are truly the best in the biz!

Last but not least- I want to thank my business partner, sister-friend, and Gemini twin, Tiffanie Mims. Thank you for making me stop and speak to you all those years ago when we first met in Diamond Hall on FAMU's campus. I am thankful for my experience at Morris Brown College in Atlanta where I received a full academic scholarship. At the time, I was committed to a relationship with my boyfriend who attended FAMU. I never would have imagined that we'd still be friends, running our business empire together after all these years. It's because of you that entrepreneurship was even a thought, cause Lord knows I never wanted to work for myself. All I wanted back then was a good-paying job with benefits and vacation time. I thank God for you, and look forward to writing our next chapter together - 20 more years!! Love ya!

XOXO Lex

Preface:
AND IN THE BEGINNING, GOD CREATED A BOSS

A smart girl knows her limits, a wise woman has none.
-Tiff & Lex-

What we're about to tell you will likely be the opposite of much of what you have been taught or learned about entrepreneurship and maybe even life in general. What we have managed to accomplish in the world of fashion and e-commerce in two decades goes against the grain and challenges the societally imposed standards of who and what the world has said that black women in business are and can be. What has become of us is the result of an indescribable cocktail. A shot of fate, a dash of destiny, and an ounce of ambition sprinkled with purpose can go a long way. This list of ingredients, when shaken and stirred and poured out over ice, has manifested in the best damn martini of life. And with every sip, there lies the presence of the pursuit of dreams and the sweet taste of success that we continue to serve up to thousands of women on a daily basis.

For the last twenty years, we have ventured to build something that was greater than each of us could have ever imagined. God had greater in store for us such that we might be empowered to walk in the absence of fear while creating a fashion empire worthy of documenting. We've broken the rules and dispelled the misconceptions on so many levels. The world has long told us that black women do not have the capacity to work together. We've been labeled as incapable of properly managing our finances. Fake news would have you to believe that we don't have the capacity to create empires. This is simply not our truth. We have resolved to reject the lies at all costs. In full disclosure, we have done quite the opposite in constructing what will be a lasting legacy of business for generations to come. Up until this point, we worked in silence and allowed our success to show up as our spokesperson.

Today, we recognize that the stories of the trials and tribulations, consecutive seasons of growth and development, and the harsh acquisition of business acumen is worthy of sharing, so that you might be empowered. We walked into the boardroom in stilettos so that the next generation of fashionpreneurs could run in spiked heels. We've felt the immense impact of pressure to acquire, cultivate and scale a business, and at times it was daunting. Ever firm believers in the truth that pressure makes diamonds, we stand uncontested and undisputed as icons in our line of business. And while some may take offense to the term, we believe and encourage women to stop being humble about the areas of life where success has been attained. Gone are the days that women are expected to apologize for greatness.

We must stand up and be recognized for the things that we are destined to do and the calling on our lives.

There comes a time when all that you have learned and every lesson that you have acquired begins to overflow. In those moments, you can not afford to sit on the expertise, years of knowledge acquired, and experiences gained. We believe that now more than ever, we have a responsibility to teach and to share and to extend our arms with love for those who aspire to this calling of fashion and business.

Along our journey, we have always remained steadfast as the personification of grit, relentless ambition and an unapologetic walk in purpose and power. It is without question that the most significant jewel in the crown of our legacy will be the way that we showed up for one another in real life and the conglomerate that we dared to build with our bare hands. Simply put, we did that shit like it has never been done before. Now it's time that we revealed how it has all been possible when the odds were stacked against us.

The pages of this book are laced with recounted stories about bad bitches in heels, real-life bosses building business, and two women on a mission to make history today. There are some people, places and things that God ordains and when he does, you simply get in place and follow his lead. Remaining steadfast and loyal to a vision that at times no one could see except us is the single most significant act that led us to this very moment. And as cliché as it may sound...we were created for a time such as this. There are some people who have limits and then there are others willing to envision a world without them. We are the latter.

XO,

Tiff & Lex

Alpha

The good friend will hold your hand. The right friend will force you to level TF up.
-Tiff and Lex-

S imply stated, she who finds a friend findeth a good thing. This theory has proven to be indisputably true for us. Over the past twenty years, we have personified the silent code of conduct that urges us to be our sister's keeper. The world would have you believe that women can't work together and that the only true way to ascend on your quest to success is to step on the next woman. This simply isn't true. Your light will never shine any brighter because you attempted to dim that of another. We've proven that two heads are better than one. In making the decision to become our own bosses, we allowed no one to dictate our beliefs about the possibilities. This meant that silencing the haters, naysayers, dream killers and non-believers was a must. In both our personal lives and careers as entrepreneurs, we managed to lean on one another as a solid foundation of support. Together we have seen the darkest hours and illuminated skies while breaking barriers and slaying stereotypes like never before. We have sustained life's tumultuous moments and the ever-growing pains of life as women in business. We've seen bankrolls larger than we ever imagined and we've conquered every moment that called us to add pressure to the hustle.

And although we dare not call this undeniably divinely ordered connection a friendship, there is no word more powerful that embodies the fullness of the unbreakable bond that was ignited and still exists between us.

TIFF

One might say that orange and green has been running through my veins since I was about ten years of age. Those colors collectively represented the prestigious Florida Agricultural and Mechanical University, known to the world as FAMU. My aunt was a student at the college during the most impressionable time in my life. My family and I often visited the campus and I loved everything about it. From the fly-ass girls walking on campus to the undeniable culture that was ever present. It was poppin! One year in particular, we went for homecoming and it was so live that my fate was solidified. The football games boasted the marching band and a sea of love that can only be described by those who have had the pleasure of experiencing it. There was no question where I wanted to go to college. I was destined to become a FAMU Rattler if it was the last thing that I did.

Eventually, my aunt graduated and also received a position at the school, which meant that she remained in the city. When she came home on her breaks, she was fly as shit. Her friends were super lit and I wanted nothing more than to be like them. By the time I got into high school and began researching the cost of college, I was made aware of the out-of-state tuition factor. Determined to realize my dream of attending FAMU, I made the decision to move from Kentucky with my mother to Florida with my aunt to complete my senior year. The move allowed me to familiarize myself with the city and to be considered for in-state tuition. I graduated with honors and a seventy-five percent academic scholarship. The scholarship and my financial aid meant that I would never have to fall victim to student loan debt, a factor that would be important to my business building later.

Moving out of my aunt's home after graduation from high school into Diamond Hall on FAMU's campus was so dope! After the first semester, a girl named Alexis who was super fly from Miami, Florida moved across the hallway from me. She rocked wigs and dope-ass earrings. The whole wig trend wasn't even a thing back then. I wondered to myself who this hot girl could have been. She had bangles poppin and door knocker earrings. I remember thinking to myself this Dade County Bitch is popping! Who does she think she is?

I loved her style and independence. We both found ourselves in the same little clique of friends and I made conversation with her, even when she appeared to be quiet. There was something in me that saw something in her. She could not have been that fashionable without some real character, even if she didn't shout it from the rooftops.

Our little clique of about six friends made plans to attend all of the major events in the city. From Kappa Luau, a massive outdoor festival hosted by Kappa Alpha Psi, Fraternity, Inc. to the Florida Classic where the entire state of Florida linked up to watch our football team battle it out against our biggest rival, Bethune Cookman University, also known as BCU (Bethune Cookman College back then). We left no stone unturned when it came to getting lit. Be Out Day was another outdoor meetup hosted by our school, and everybody who was anybody on the campus and in the city of Tallahassee, Florida was on site.

We all made plans to travel together and to play as hard as we worked. Over time, Alexis and I discovered that no matter how much planning we did with the group, the two of us always ended up following through, simply because we managed our coins. She had her money and was ready to go and I had mine. There was something different about the way we handled bank than the other girls in the group. This factor drew us even closer. And then there were two.

LEX

Growing up in Florida meant that I had no intention of attending school in the state. In an attempt to venture out, I made the decision to attend Morris Brown College in Atlanta. The city was popping but I was dating a guy who attended FAMU. As much as we tried to make phone calls and periodic visits work, it wasn't enough. As a self-proclaimed introvert, I had not made any friendships that were worthy of additional investment. After my first semester, I made the decision to transfer to the school that my boyfriend was attending.

When I reached *THE HILL*, as we affectionately called the school, I was assigned a dorm room in Diamond Hall. The all-female dorm was a bustling home to many of the freshman girls on campus. Many of my dorm-mates had already forged friendships, as they had been attending the school together the previous semester. My routine entailed attending class and returning to my room to chill. That was until one day, an energetic young lady named Tiffanie began speaking to me routinely in passing. Our rooms were across the hall from each other, so our interactions were frequent.

One day in particular, she decided to strike up a full-blown conversation. Per usual, I was extending my one-word answers but she was not allowing me to get away without giving more to the conversation. The more we talked, the more we realized how much we had in common. We both loved to shop, travel and most importantly, track our coins. Once I recognized that Tiffanie was as much about her business and leveling up as me, it was game over!

A WORD TO THE WISE

The next time you hear someone utter the words that women can't get along, be sure to give them the side-eye. This book is proof that we've been lied to all along. The real truth is that we are more powerful together than we could ever be apart. That old adage that teamwork makes the dream work is based on a true story.

And whether you make the decision to tackle a dream alone or in partnership, you must first discover how to be whole. The secret sauce for us has been the fact that neither of us were broken or non-believers in the magic and the power of what we dared to do together. We both knew without question that if we worked and pledged our allegiance to the grind, that we had the power to will what our wildest imagination could only dream of. Together, we learned that we were not fragile like flowers—we were fragile like bombs. Doing business became our plan to set shit off!

I:
THE BOOK OF AMBITION

**The world does not owe you anything
that you are not willing to work for.**
-Tiff & Lex-

If you are looking for anything that resembles an easy path to success, it is suggested that you close this book immediately and pass it along to someone who is not afraid of hard work. Creating a boutique that withstands the test of time requires stamina and passion that burns long after the thrill of the glitz and glamour that often precedes this business.

TIFF

I've always been the girl that was willing to work for *it*, and by *it*, I mean any goal that I deemed worthy of my time, energy and intention. Even as a child, my ambition was rooted in what I dared to accomplish. Betting on myself was the move. Managing every dollar and responsible oversight of my cash flow was never optional for me. In college at FAMU, when I received my net check, I never blew my money on frivolous things. I did not go shopping or throw parties with the money that was granted to me for my education. Unlike most of my friends, I had real responsibility on my shoulders that included sending money back home to help my mother.

Since the age of sixteen, I had maintained employment, and college was no different. My job at U-Haul as a sales representative proved to be a lick. Not only did U-Haul have good working hours, but my pay rate was bomb. I was banking almost $1250 per month, which is amazing for a college student. The U-Haul facility in which I worked was not far from the airport. On my way to work each day, I passed by the rental car companies that were situated along the same road. After learning about the benefits and hours the rental car companies offered to their employees, seeking my next position with one of these companies became a no-brainer. Once I set my sights on getting a job of this caliber, I was persistent as hell. Stopping in to the business office each day and inquiring about the opportunities that they had available was a part of my schedule. Making the necessary connections and networking came second nature to me. Eventually, I landed a job of my own with the rental car company and it was exactly what I'd imagined it to be.

I was a quick study and learned their processes and procedures with ease. Sitting behind the counter reinforced valuable lessons such as the need to maintain good credit and proper management of money. It was easy for me to observe the fact that the levels of access and freedom that people could attain was based upon their financial situation. The better their credit, the better their chances were for renting a car, while others who did not pass the credit score left empty-handed. Due to the fact that our offices were located near the airport and not inside, there was a level of leniency that we had the liberty to offer. The relaxed policies also meant that we received our fair share of the D-boys who frequented the business. D-boys switched up their cars like clockwork when they made runs or trips out of town.

In the South, you often see a lot of flash. Gold grills, neon colors, dreadlocks dipped in bronze on the ends and donks are all of the tell-tale signs. You can spot a D-boy from miles away. I knew them all and did what I could to help them handle their business at the rental counter. One client in particular piqued my interest. At first glance, you might not have known that he was a D-boy. His swag wasn't loud, it was discreet. Instead of gold grills, he had gold Cartier frames and instead of driving a donk, he had a Honda Accord that he kept glistening like new. You can learn a lot about a person and how they manage their finances when they rent a car. At the counter, he always chose the extras like premium insurance and fuel in advance. He maintained a credit card with space available on it, so it was apparent that he attended to the details of his finances. His demeanor was calm and not pressed like the others who frequented the office. He wasn't anxious and took his time when attending to his financial affairs. He was different, and my interest was piqued. The more he came into the office, the more intrigued I became with who he was and how he moved. Our interactions grew in nature and what was once an exchange of paperwork now became an exchange of energy. A random conversation at the counter led to the evolution of an exchange that would become a part of my story in more ways than one.

LEX

Making the decision to transfer from Morris Brown College in Atlanta, Georgia to attend FAMU in Tallahassee, Florida during the middle of my freshman year was laced with what some might have considered to be a touch of insanity. I was abandoning my full tuition scholarship because I was in love, and the long-distance relationship was no longer an option. When I arrived back in Florida, I had not even been officially accepted to FAMU. My name was not listed on any enrollment documents, nor was I officially registered for classes. All I had was the will to win. There was never a question in my mind whether or not there would be room made for me. I was a gifted student and I knew that I would be an asset to the school's academic excellence. Upon my arrival, I can remember going to the Registrar's Office and simply telling them that they had to find some classes for me. This is not to say that I thought that I was better than anyone else; I just believed and visualized myself in the highest capacity possible and I trusted that God had a plan for me on that campus. As they say, "He's an on-time God," because he delivered. That day, I received my schedule and classes were to commence days later.

Getting acclimated back to Florida and my relationship with my then-boyfriend happened with ease. I settled into the life that I had created in my mind and watched it materialize before my eyes. I worked hard and played hard when moments for socialization presented themselves, but never lost sight of the ultimate goal, which was graduating on time.

As my love life blossomed, so did my academic standing. About two years into my enrollment at FAMU, I found myself wanting to pursue another layer for my academia and made the decision to transfer again, this time to Florida State University (FSU). Situated just across the city, I was not far from all that had become familiar on FAMU's campus. FSU offered another experience to add to my educational repertoire. And although I was now a student enrolled in classes at FSU, FAMU could have never been replaced in my heart. I had made all of my friends and acquaintances on that campus and I returned every chance I got.

There are some parts of our lives that are meant to last forever and others that we must appreciate in their rightful season. The four-year relationship that I moved back to Florida in pursuit of took its final bow, eventually ending in a very difficult break-up. The more I grew as a young woman chasing dreams, the wider the gap became between us. At the end of the day, I will always agree that it is better to have loved and lost than to have never loved at all.

READER'S NOTE:

By now, you might be wondering what our personal relationships have to do with the story of building our businesses, but trust that if you keep reading, you will understand better by and by. The key here is that no matter what happened amidst our personal relationships, our ambition was never compromised. Relationships will experience highs and lows, but goals are not concerned with your personal life. To win also means to sacrifice yourself, and at times your feelings, until you hit your intended target. The intended target has moved over the years to greater but the goal of making money and being our own bosses has never changed. Govern yourselves accordingly.

Verse I:
CONFIDENCE

The ultimate measure of your confidence is demonstrated by your ability to trust yourself.
-Tiff & Lex-

*O*ur college years were filled with fond memories. We were the personification of balance. No matter how hard we worked, we knew how to recenter and get lit just enough to maintain our sanity. When graduation rolled around, major decisions had to be made about what the next steps would be. After pondering the obvious concepts of graduate school vs employment, we both decided that freedom was what we were really after. The only viable option that either of us saw to become our own bosses was entrepreneurship. At the time, the prospect of forgoing a traditional path to pursue something that neither of us could see was not the norm. Everyone around us was graduating and getting jobs in the fields that they had worked so hard to earn their degrees in. Meanwhile, we were plotting and planning to prosper by way of a dream that no one could see except us. And in the early stages, even we had no idea how that dream would manifest or what it would cost us in blood, sweat, and tears to bring to fruition.

With limited information, we began to scout franchise opportunities. With no prior experience with franchises, we had our work cut out for us and a vast learning curve to overcome. During that era, especially in the state of Florida, the Tropical Smoothie franchise was booming. We kept seeing locations pop up all over the place, even in the city of Tallahassee where we resided. In our minds, the prevalence of the stores was a clear indication of the business model's success. Our research also helped us to discover that opening a store of this type was within our reach. We began taking meetings with the Tropical Smoothie franchise teams to learn more. The more we learned, the more we set our intentions toward making this our company of choice. During the final stages of the decision-making process, we began scouting buildings and reading all of the fine print. Our scrutiny of the decision to join the franchise helped us to better understand what would be expected of us in running such an entity. In the end, we decided against opening a Tropical Smoothie franchise because it truly felt as though we were buying a job. The franchise fees were enormous, and the roles that we would need to execute were laborious. We both decided that if we were going to pay a business a significant amount of money to participate, it might as well be our own.

Verse II:
TRUST YOUR
INSTINCTS

**If you are in search of your purpose, discover
your passion: the two go hand in hand.**
-Tiff & Lex-

The most powerful thing that you can do when you reach a fork in the road of your life is to be still and listen to God and to the divine messages that the universe is waiting to share with you. For us, listening meant becoming aware of things that we were doing without thinking about them. On more occasions than we care to count, we visited Miami (Alexis' hometown) and the one sport that always piqued our interest was shopping! A trend that we both had been quietly paying attention to was the popular $10 shoe stores. In Miami, it was as if the $10 shoe stores had the same appeal as the Tropical Smoothie franchise that we had once considered. These stores seemed to be in every nook and cranny of the city. Traveling to Miami meant an open invitation to shop and shoes were at the top of both of our lists. We would return to Tallahassee with more pairs of shoes than we had the capacity to fit into our luggage. Fashion was a passion, and no look was complete without the right shoe. After countless conversations and brainstorming sessions, we stumbled upon the idea of opening a shoe store of our own.

From the moment that we made the decision to open a $10 shoe store of our own, we committed everything to making the dream our reality. We had compromised the opportunity to go to graduate school, and neither of us had taken the role of employment in the traditional sense, which also meant that we could only rely on each other.

After securing silent investors in the form of a thriving relationship with a D-boy and parents, we managed to raise a little under seven thousand dollars to launch the business. With financial backing in place, the next order of business was scouting a location. Our goal was to set up residence in a venue where we could see immediate traffic and benefit from the action. The obvious contender for retail therapy was the mall. When we discussed the idea it became real, which also empowered us to allow it to evolve into an achievable goal. With our hearts set on opening our first location in the Governor's Square Mall, the most heavily visited mall in Tallahassee, we made moves quickly. And while for some, taking a risk of this magnitude would have been scary, we were simply motivated. There was something about opening a shoe store that gave us a sense of confidence.

We were the customer and the target audience, thus it would have been hard to not know what the customer liked, which also meant that we had the capacity to make sales. If you are not willing to bet on yourself, ask yourself, who shall?

Verse III:
TRIAL AND ERROR

**It is possible to be in search of
something that you already have.**
-Tiff & Lex-

The next order of business could have been coined *Operation Spend Money to Make Money!* Our only goal was to become profitable, and we recognized that getting our hands on as much inventory as possible to sell and establish a source of income was the priority. We made the decision to rent a U-Haul truck and return to Miami to purchase as many pairs of shoes as we could with a budget of approximately three thousand dollars, the money left after all of the other expenses to finance the startup were completed. We believed that if we hit up enough ten dollar shoe stores, we could score a major win for our store.

When we arrived in Miami, we made the decision to make a pit stop at a local flea market to check out options for inventory and discovered several pairs of shoes that we loved and viewed as good additions for the store. Just as we began to experience a sense of enthusiasm about the moves that we were making, we learned that there was a trade show happening in Miami the exact same weekend. The next day, we set our sights on attending the trade show to explore more inventory potentials. As we strolled through the aisles of vendors, we began to recognize many of the pairs of shoes that we had purchased from the flea market for full price the previous day displayed at a wholesale rate. That day, we learned that we had been bamboozled at the flea market. We'd paid double what we should have actually paid. It hurt like hell to know that the man at the flea market had taken advantage of us, but the bigger lesson was rooted in the value of attending trade shows to select and purchase inventory. There was no vendor list or easy way to find distributors in the industry back then because vendors did not have websites yet and did not exist online. Wiser and more attuned to product vs. profit margins, we made smart purchases at the trade show. We also bought some used store fixtures, as we knew that we still had the task of creating the store layout.

The next day, we packed up the U-Haul and made the seven-hour drive back to Tallahassee. Taking the drive back home made us realize that we were wiser, filled with vision and possessing an opportunity for success. You can either wait for your dream to unfold, or you can work for it. We chose the latter.

Prophecies and
REVELATIONS

*E*very moment of our lives can be categorized as a success or failure, depending on how you choose to see it. We believe that if a lesson can be acquired, no moment is a failure. Every ounce of information that you stand to gain is a solid opportunity for your advancement. Being charged double for the first inventory that we purchased taught us about the endless possibilities for marking up products in our industry. In the same spirit, we struck gold when we purchased a few cases of boots that cost us only $3 per pair and retailed them at $55 a pair and they sold. We would not have known to handle our potential profit in this way had we not been gifted the experience of being overcharged at that flea market. Instead of wading in what feels like disappointment, seeking to thrive amidst the prospect of opportunity and destiny is far more fruitful.

Divine Intervention:
STRENGTH FINDER

*O*ne major way to channel your inner confidence is to get laser-focused on the things that you do well. Knowing without question where your strengths lie will help you to position yourself for business. Use the space below to write an "S" for strength or "D" for developmental in each of the entrepreneurship traits listed below.

___ **Ambition**
___ **Creativity**
___ **Intelligence**
___ **Curiosity**
___ **Leadership**
___ **Empathy**
___ **Honesty**
___ **Logic**
___ **Gratitude**

An Affirmation
OF AMBITION

I AM becoming more driven each day.

My focus is increasingly stronger.

Obstacles will not define me.

I will work relentlessly.

I will achieve what I will.

I will become what I envision.

My Reflections

_____

_____

_____

_____

_____

_____

_____

_____

_____

_____

_____

_____

_____

_____

_____

_____

_____

My Reflections

My Reflections

My Reflections

_____

_____

_____

_____

_____

_____

_____

_____

_____

_____

_____

_____

_____

_____

_____

_____

_____

_____

My Reflections

II:
THE BOOK OF VISION

If you can master the art of seeing what is not visible, then you have vision.

-Tiff & Lex-

Scared money can't make money. If you are making plans to pursue entrepreneurship in any form, there will be moments in which faith in the things hoped for will be your greatest asset. It is not possible to predict the circumstances or outcomes that you will encounter along this journey. It is imperative that you always remember why you started and vow to put one foot in front of the other, even on the days when you are too tired to walk. Remember, when you walk in purpose, God will not only order your steps, but he will also carry you.

TIFF

Walking into the next phase of life, I felt like a boss! My relationship with the D-boy was alive and well. As time grew, he continued to witness how I handled my business and I watched him with an even closer eye. One weekend in particular, he expressed the need to cut our time together short because he needed to go out and make money. Although I was aware of what he did, I was not directly involved with his business endeavours.

In response to him needing to leave, I asked him, "How much money do you need?" He looked at me as if he had seen a ghost as I awaited his response. My continued gaze let him know that I was serious. "I guess like $1200 to finish off the weekend," he replied. "Oh. Well, I have $1200 in the bank that I can loan you, so that you don't have to leave." Even more shocked and surprised by my words, he just continued to gaze. "Just stay here. I'll run to the bank and pick it up," I said as I grabbed my keys.

By the time I returned, he was sitting in the same place that I'd left him, as if the aftermath of my words were still with him. I tossed the money on the table. "Here you go. Just give it back to me when you can."

The smirk on his face let me know that he would soon break his silence. "Wow, Tiff. I mean, I've just never been able to count on anybody except myself. Most of the women that I have dated have always looked for me to help them. I can't lie. That shit is dope." He leapt up from the couch and came over to me, placing his hands on my shoulders. "Listen to me. You are different. You just showed me a lot about who you are. We are about to change shit up for real. From now on, fuck them Christian Dior bags. I don't want us to talk about materialistic shit like bags and shoes and shit. We about to be on another level. From now on, we are only discussing houses and investments because I can tell that you can get with this shit. I'm about to put you on to some game."

His words stuck with me because even though I didn't know exactly what he had in mind, I was completely in alignment with the concept of leveling up on some business shit. In my lifetime I have desired to be many things but broke has never been one of them.

D-boy stayed true to his word and we purchased our first home together when I was just twenty years of age. He also made the decision to invest in the business once again after seeing how Alexis and I began to prove that we were on one with moving our businesses forward.

LEX

Tiffanie and I were on the verge of something amazing as we prepared to launch the shoe store. We attempted to think of every angle and to devise a plan to accommodate the needs for the launch. Making the decision not to go to graduate school and open the business meant that I could only count on myself and the work that Tiffanie and I created together. There was no plan B, so I was not willing to allow our plan to fail on my watch.

Not only was our seed funding non-traditional but it was also minimal in comparison to the size of the dream that we were attempting to fund. We implemented strategy and stretched the money as far and wide as possible to get the business off the ground. The first expenditure that we executed was the deposit for the store in the mall that we'd set our intentions toward. After securing a location, we moved forward with acquiring insurance and we also hired an attorney to manage the oversight of the creation of our business entity. We also hired a CPA to set up all of our accounts. They didn't manage money but secured a structure for us to implement sound financial practices. We set a budget and monitored every penny like hawks. After the store opened, we never actually spoke about reinvesting every dollar back into the business, but we did.

We premeditated the process of setting up our business the right way and left no stone unturned in the paperwork. To generate a buzz, we purchased small advertising spots on the local radio station and a minimal amount of flyers for distribution. At the time, these methods were the best ways to reach consumers on the ground.

To display the inventory, we bought stands and fixtures. To save money, we got creative by spray painting the used fixtures we purchased to give them a makeover and pieced as many decorative items that we could together. From small embellished what-nots to mirrors, we did all the things within a minimal budget to make the store come together aesthetically. After a period of thirty days, we were officially open for business. The next month's rent was on our ass and we were adamant about making sure that we could meet it.

Even though I approached the launch of the store with anticipation for what we had the capability to produce, never in a million years could I have predicted all that would manifest. Violet Haze, named for its purple walls and overall motif, was officially open for business.

Verse I:
THE BLUEPRINT

**Whatsoever you aim for in life,
you are sure to hit it.**
-Tiff & Lex-

*A*fter our grand opening, we got down to business building. At the time, we didn't realize that we had managed to secure our own niche in the marketplace. There were not any other stores in the city that offered what we had. After two short months of business, we had earned enough to pay back our silent investors. And because of the way that we were moving shoes like weight, D-boy made another investment to make sure that we were able to stock more inventory. We were moving shoes by the pound.

After the trials and tribulations of baptism by fire in Miami, we now worked to establish relationships with vendors that we could trust. Our South Florida vendors' reps would make the seven hour drive from Miami to our store with samples and their catalogs and we had the liberty to choose what we knew our customers would receive as fire. The sales rep would write up the order and get everything shipped to us for sale and distribution. Pumps, heels, wedges, boots in every color that a girl could consider kept the ladies coming back to the store. We were what the city had been missing. It should also be noted that there was no e-commerce at the time, which pushed more customers our way. The level of exclusivity that we managed to set in motion also set us up to charge what we deemed profitable for our shoes because there was nothing else for customers to compare it to. We were smart buyers who managed to corner the market.

The trade show in Miami had also taught us the importance of attending to learn firsthand about new merchandise offerings and to make the selections for ourselves. Traveling to trade shows in Atlanta, Miami, Las Vegas and New York was now a customary routine and even as time progressed, we would not send buyers in our place; we showed up to make the best decisions about every detail for our company and customers. Success is often in the details that are unseen or taken for granted by most people, but our secret sauce has always been rooted in the intricacies.

We left no stone unturned when it came to the branding and marketing for the business. We even went as far as to disguise the fact that we were the owners. Although sad to say, we didn't want to lose the support of any potential customers because of the fact that we were two young, black girls who had launched a business of this magnitude. Instead of answering questions about our identity, we instead put our emphasis into constructing a solid framework for the business to thrive. Not only were we focused on the details, but we also remained in alignment with the vision that we'd created for ourselves prior to launching.

To ensure that we were properly staffed, we interviewed and hired new team members. Even though we had help, we showed up for work on a daily basis to satisfy our assigned shifts and to ensure that things were running properly. And while many may feel as though you don't need to be present if you have someone working for you, that was not the case for us. We believed that if we showed up, then the work done in the store would be at an optimal level. Waking up to go to a job hits differently when it is one that you have created for yourself. Neither of us had retail experience, which also meant that we were in training while running the business.

One specific strategy that many businesses in the city leveraged was to hire college students who needed employment. We went after the girls that were super cute that we knew our customers would find attractive. This strategy enhanced the buyer experience and elevated the brand. And as easy as it sounds to hire a college student, it was not without challenges. Turnover of staff was high and there were times that some members were unreliable, which further proved the need for us to be present on a consistent basis. We hired girls of all races, colors and creeds and they attracted our ideal customers. Another challenge during this era was that we were the same age as the young ladies that we hired. It was often difficult for them to see us as their superiors because we were their peers. We had a business to run so we always found a way to triumph. After our first six months of being in operation, we both knew that Violet Haze was much bigger than we could have ever imagined it to be.

Verse II:
IF YOU BUILD IT, THEY WILL COME

The goal in life is to build something greater than yourself and a legacy that will extend beyond your years.

-Tiff & Lex-

I f we didn't know that we'd landed on a gold mine after taking a leap of faith into entrepreneurship to create Violet Haze, there was no question after the first FAMU Homecoming. Homecoming at one of the most prestigious historically black universities cannot be put into words. The droves of people both local and from afar who attend can't be quantified. The feelings of nostalgia and even the air of the city is different during homecoming season. There is an uncanny sense of excitement and reunion which results in the ultimate fellowship of alumni and the entire city.

Upon our first homecoming after opening Violet Haze, we didn't quite know what to expect. All we knew was that the mall stayed lit. This also meant that if we played our cards right we had a prime opportunity to sell lots of shoes! That year, in true homecoming fashion, the streets were closed off. You couldn't even get to the mall, but of course those who wanted to be there got creative and found their way around the roadblocks. Before the game and after the game, the mall was crowded from corner to corner with people, so much so that it was like a club. Everybody who was anybody found a way to be in the building. This had been the case for many years and there were even times that the crowd turned into a stampede, but on this day more people made more traffic, which equaled more business.

Our strategy of having super cute employees worked to our benefit. We had also created an environment in the store that made people want to just hang out. We kept the music bumping so people didn't mind hanging around. The ladies were there to check out the shoes and grab their outfits for the club that night, and the fellas were there to check out the ladies. The dudes that wanted to prove their baller status spent money on shoes, and we didn't mind one bit. We experienced a few thefts but they paled in comparison to the profit made that weekend. When it was all said and done, we consolidated the books to determine the sales from the weekend. We were beyond shocked at what we discovered.

In less than 48 hours we had managed to sell enough shoes to deposit over $50,000 in the bank. We were fresh out of college, running a small, closet-sized storefront with a basic cash register that we purchased from Office Depot and had managed to clear more in two days than some of the existing storefronts with larger staff and those experienced in retail could clear in six months. At the time, there was no social media, no widespread messaging on the world wide web, now known as the internet, no telephone orders and no major marketing budget. Every single dollar that we made over that two-day period was from customers who had come into the store to spend their hard-earned money on the shoes that we had selected for our inventory. What we accomplished was monumental. Imagine the tears that we both held back after crossing such a major hurdle in such a short period of time. We had been in business for less than a year and made more money than some businesses make in years. It was unbelievable. Looking at our accounts, it felt like someone had deposited dope money. It felt like we had discovered the best leak that ever existed. From that moment on we both knew that we had been granted access to an exclusive club and this wasn't the dope game: this was shoes. Neither of us had ever had that much money in our bank accounts at one time. There were a series of emotions that we both experienced, everything from being frightened to excited to crying tears of joy. Prior to the large profit in that short period of time, we had always paid ourselves very humbly, but on that day we both deserved a small bonus.

Still functioning from a place of responsibility, we allotted ourselves ten grand apiece and vowed to reinvest the rest back into the business. A few days later we found ourselves at the car dealership in search of two cars that looked like they were for the boys but really they were for us. We had done the work and we deserved to floss the way we wanted to, and so we did. The cars were brand new off the lot. One Chevy Impala, and one Monte Carlo Super Sport. If you saw us roll up in the parking lot you would have assumed that it was two dudes, but as soon as the car doors opened you would've easily recognized that it was two boss bitches.

Verse III:
PREPARE FOR INCREASE

**Make a living and leave a
footprint when you leave.**
-Tiff & Lex-

The fifty thousand dollar homecoming weekend resulted in exponential growth for Violet Haze. We used the money to purchase more inventory, solidify staff, and restructure marketing efforts to increase sales. The growth of the boutique now required more space, as we were running out of room for our inventory. The Violet Haze store space resembled a large walk-in closet; it might have been seven to eight hundred square feet total in size. After much thought and consideration, we made the decision to take the business plan that had worked and proven to be effective and launch a second location in the same mall. We worked extremely hard to build relationships with the management staff at the mall and conferred with them about the prospect of a new store. The mall's management team was both encouraging and prepared to strategize and help us make the dream of opening a second location a reality.

We found ourselves faced with the challenge of coming up with another name and also determining how the second store would differ from the first. One of the names thrown into the hat for consideration was BellaDonna. The term meant *beautiful woman* in Italian. The space that they showed us was three times the size of Violet Haze. This time, we had the ability to purchase 100% of the new inventory on credit. Our vendors were now extending us 30-60 day payment terms. The key to scaling a business is making sure that you have the processes and procedures in place for the first time to effectively duplicate your efforts. We had done the work to create Violet Haze and we were up for the challenge of launching BellaDonna Shoes.

Although we would be carrying shoes by the same brand and our vendors had not changed, the goal for this store was to appeal to a more mature, sexier audience. Everything from the selection of shoes to the aesthetic of the store was looks. We stocked the store with every style of shoe in every color available. At first, we weren't geeked about the actual location as it was located near the entrance of the mall and the bus stop.

We were determined to make the best of our location and we did. What we did not know was how we would be affected by having two stores in motion simultaneously. The only thing that was for certain was our ambition.

In true entrepreneurial fashion, we also considered scaling the business once more. After recognizing that the infrastructure that we'd created did a significant profit margin and mastering the start-up approach, we knew that we had a solid strategy to launch our business in a similar setting. We worked for months to follow the same steps toward success for BellaDonna as we had for Violet Haze. The store was fully stocked, fully furnished, and fully equipped for customers. The concept of establishing a buying space for a new audience took off just as we had imagined. There we were, two young women under the age of 30 running two majorly successful shoe boutiques in the epicenter of the mall in the state's capital. Business was booming once again and we were witnessing another bout of exponential growth right before our eyes.

And just when we settled in to the notion of expansion, and after months of relentless toil, we received a blow by some earth-shattering news. The ladies from the mall's leasing office, whom we had maintained a positive relationship with, paid a visit to the store. It was apparent from the looks on their faces that they had not come bearing good news. To our surprise. they told us that we would be forced to close down Violet Haze because the space was now being acquired by a local NFL celebrity, who was opening a sports apparel store. Apparently he had purchased one section of a space but needed our space as well to ensure enough capacity for his inventory and foot traffic. Based upon the contractual agreement, the ladies did not have to inform us. It was in response to the positive relationship that we had established with them that we were even given a heads-up. Contractually they weren't required to disclose this information to us and we were required to give up the space. This dilemma was one of the major pitfalls of leasing retail space in a major mall.

At the time the looks on our faces must've said it all. We were devastated. Our only hope was to try to acquire another space in a different location. We were informed that the entire mall was full and there were no other retail spaces available for us to lease.

In a desperate scramble for an answer, we told them that we needed another store. They had nowhere to move us. The lesson was that sometimes you need to maximize the space that you are working with. That evening we left feeling defeated. There were so many questions that we did not have answers for. What would happen to all of our inventory? Where would we move the inventory to? Would we lose all of our business? Would our customers be able to find us? Would we lose profits and all of the momentum that we had worked so hard to attain? Why had this happened to us? The move had to happen in a swift fashion and we were left with no other option except to call in help with the relocation of the glass fixtures and all of the inventory that lined the walls of the chic boutique with the purple walls. Closing Violet Haze was depressing and it felt like we'd suffered a tremendous loss.

With nowhere else to store the inventory, we arranged for it to be brought to the BellaDonna location.

While standing there at the entrance of BellaDonna, we watched the glass fixtures and the shoes pour into the store. In that moment, something magical happened. The walls of the store that had once looked slightly sparse were now being filled with life and inventory. It was a spiritual experience in a sense because what we had once felt to be the greatest decrease and punishment from God actually revealed itself as a blessing in disguise. The greatest lesson that we learned was to refrain from being so emotionally tied to our business and redirect our emotions toward strategy. We also knew that if we believed in God and trusted what He has for us, then He would see us through.

With every passing month, the revenue for BellaDonna tripled. Sometimes the answer to your request to grow is simply to maximize the space that you are already working with.

Prophecies and REVELATIONS

*Y*ou have to learn when to hold them and when to fold them. There are times that we attempt to hold on to things of lesser value when God desires to bless us with greater.

The most important thing that an entrepreneur can do for themselves is to create their own luck. Both opportunity and a will to win must be present at all times for destiny to take shape. Forward progression cannot occur in the absence of action. Even the best laid plans fall through. It is imperative when building business to remain a constant student of the procedures, processes and people that drive the climate and continuity of your business.

Entrepreneurs must also be fearless in their efforts. If you are not willing to bet on yourself, how can you ever expect anyone else to believe in you? Be willing to bet big and realize big wins. It is equally important to remove your ego from the equation.

There is no profit in working only to stake a claim to power. Know your roles and the consistent activities that you engage in to bring about prosperity for your business and be of good integrity and truthful about everything that unfolds. Remember to leave pettiness and anything that resembles it at the front door. Your business can only thrive when your heart and soul are free to soar.

Divine Intervention:
MASTERING
THE ART OF
RESILIENCY

*D*on't try to solve problems with the same thinking that created them. Resilient people do not make the same mistake over and over again. Those who can survive the storms of life and business and come out stronger on the other side are willing to be honest about why they might not have succeeded the first time and they take the time to think about factors that did or didn't work.

What is a current problem that you currently need to solve with a different way of thinking?

_____

_____

An Affirmation
OF INNOVATION

Genius is in my DNA.

I am an incubator for new ideas.

My work ethic will be a catalyst for my dreams.

Illuminated paths will guide me toward success.

My Reflections

_____

_____

_____

_____

_____

_____

_____

_____

_____

_____

_____

_____

_____

_____

_____

_____

_____

My Reflections

My Reflections

My Reflections

My Reflections

_____

_____

_____

_____

_____

_____

_____

_____

_____

_____

_____

_____

_____

_____

_____

_____

_____

III:
THE BOOK OF
DETERMINATION

There are no shortcuts when walking
up the stairway to heaven.
-Tiff & Lex-

To be in business is not to exist in the shadows waiting to be discovered. Being in business dictates that you create a flag that is so colorful and so profoundly exquisite that your people can see it in the distance and discover you. You must tell them why they need you and make it clear how you can help. As a business owner, you must be the solution to someone's problem. If solving problems for others is not your reason for existence, what else could it be?

TIFF

We had our eyes set on expansion. And even though the last attempt had not panned out the way that we intended, I knew in my heart that more doors were preparing to open for us.

In spite of everything that had transpired, the boutique business reflected rays of sunlight. My personal life, on the other hand, had seen brighter days.

So many moments with D-boy made me question if I was the only woman in his life. From the time when we met at the counter of my job at the car rental center to the years that we spent together, I never doubted that I was his chosen one. My intuition began to lead me down a path of curiosity that at some point killed the cat. Now, a little more mature, a little wiser and a little more financially independent as entrepreneurs, Lex and I took a trip to Atlanta for Super Bowl weekend. All the ballers were there and the city was lit!

When we arrived, I called D-boy to let him know that we were there and he had the hotel set up for us. Just as we pulled up, he arrived with his homeboy. The four of us chilled for a bit in the room and just kicked it. About thirty minutes into us being there, he stood up and told me that he had to go. I was confused. Like what the fuck would he need to go do that didn't involve spending time with me on a big weekend like this? At the time, I felt like we were getting ready to ball out the entire weekend together. The look in his eyes let me know that there was nothing that I could have said to prevent him from leaving in that moment. His homeboy stood up and said his goodbyes and they were out.

If I had ever doubted that there was someone else, that day served as confirmation. The only problem was that I didn't have absolute proof of anything. The way he moved was so strategic that I didn't really see shit. In hindsight, that could have been the day that I accepted the fact that I was sharing my man with someone else. And while I could have tricked myself into believing that him leaving was about getting money, I had done that many times before. That moment in Atlanta, standing in the middle of the room with my pride at my feet was my dance with the truth. He didn't need to confirm shit. For a while I had been Stevie Wonder to the bullshit but on that day, even I couldn't turn a blind eye. I already had all the information that I needed. The bigger question became what would I do with the truth?

After that weekend ended, I was like any woman who discovers that her man has dealings outside of the relationship. I was part salty and part jealous. Whenever he tried to leave, I had questions, more than I had ever asked before. He was not used to me being in that headspace, nor was I. In many ways, I felt that I no longer had control of my heart and that shit hurt like hell. One day, he was leaving the house and something inside of me mustered up the strength to ask the one question that I never really wanted him to answer: "Who is she?"

To this day, I'm not sure what made me ask so directly. Please believe that whatever you seek, you will get that shit, and trust, I did.

"Listen. We can't keep doing this. I have someone in Atlanta. That is home. There is nothing that I can do about it. It's not going to change. I just need to keep that separate from what we are doing here." Those were his words. He confirmed what I already knew. My heart hurt because I had invested so much time into this man. I had already given him years. We now had multiple houses together, and cars and all kinds of other shit. Most importantly, I was entangled emotionally in his web. I had fallen in love with him and saw us having a future together. It was fucked up that he conveniently decided to put me up on game that I was the sidechick.

All I could say in the moment was "Are you married?" As fucked up as it is, that was what I felt I had as the only leverage toward a deal breaker.

"No," he replied solemnly.

"I mean, what the fuck? Like, why didn't you tell me this shit?" I went ballistic in a rage and began pacing back and forth with my hands squeezing my head. He grabbed me from behind and held me tighter than he ever had. The warmth of his arms calmed me. Standing there felt like the home that we had been building together. We stood there in silence for what felt like an eternity and just like that, I let that shit go. Just like that, even though I spoke no words, I had agreed to be the other woman.

LEX

I've always believed in keeping my heart open as I move throughout the world and in life in general. My belief is that remaining open to love in all things is the only way to gain access to the abundance that life has to offer. If we close ourselves off, these things have no way of discovering us in an already crowded world with everyone vying for attention. In this space, I don't have to search for love, it finds me. I was most open to the prospect of love not long after we opened the store.

Walking away peacefully from the relationship that I had outgrown several years prior allowed me quiet time to search for myself. I discovered that the most powerful version of me was the one who chased dreams and made no apologies for it. Anyone or anything that could not align with where I was trying to go became an afterthought. God sent me those who would align with what I believed his mission for my life became and I was ready to welcome them with open arms.

One day I was standing at the register in the store and I noticed a gentleman walk by. As fate would have it, our eyes connected from far away. On another occasion, he came into the store and struck up a conversation. We must have stood there talking about nothing for at least thirty minutes. I can't even recall if any customers came into the store during that time but if they did, I'm sure they helped themselves because I was giddy. I got used to seeing him because he would pop up at the mall often and of course he knew where to find me. During one of our random conversations, one thing led to another and he asked me to go on a date. It was an easy *yes* for me because I did enjoy his company. He was funny and attractive but most importantly, I could feel my heart smiling when I was in his presence, which let me know that there was something there.

The seasons changed but our constant communication did not. He would frequently visit me at work and after work we would go out together for dinner. We shared chemistry and got lost in each other's company. Time seemed to stand still and I knew in my heart that I had found my person. As the months rolled by, we made the decision to create a life together. He proposed to me and with a glimmer of love in my heart and in my eyes, I said yes! Now, in anticipation of the life I had dreamed of and amidst the elevation of business I had worked so hard for, life was good.

Verse I:
SEEK AND YE
SHALL FIND

The storms of life require your best umbrellas.
-Tiff & Lex-

*O*pening Violet Haze and BellaDonna taught us that you are only as good as your next business move in motion. Adamant, empowered and intuitive about the need to make another move, we began to set our intent to open another location into the atmosphere. Atlanta, Houston, Savannah and Montgomery were among the cities that we began scouting in an attempt to recreate the magic that we'd created in the city of Tallahassee. The mall in Montgomery had the perfect size space and was within the allotted budget that we agreed upon for the new store. The city was only a three-hour drive from Tallahassee, which meant that we had easy access to get back and forth. Montgomery was also home of Tuskegee University, which encouraged our thinking that there would be a similar dynamic that FAMU had to Tallahassee.

All things considered, it was a great location. We hosted the store's grand opening approximately two months after confirming the location.

As crazy as it sounds today, while still new business owners, we were not thinking about branding and expanding the recognition of one of the brands that we'd created even though we were attempting to duplicate the same business model. We discovered that people were getting tongue tied with the name BellaDonna, so we opted for a simpler approach and named the third location Pretty & Chic. The sign that we had made said Pretty & Chic and had the silhouette of a black woman on it. We didn't even ask any questions; we just went with it.

The mall was open from 10 am to 9 pm Monday through Saturday and noon to 6 pm on Sunday. Our goal was to rotate time at each of the stores in both cities to ensure that there was always coverage. We rented a furnished apartment so that one of us could remain in Montgomery for a week at a time. In accordance with our old business plan, we stocked the inventory with approximately fifteen thousand dollars in products. Channeling our same blueprint for success, we purchased the same products for Montgomery that we had for the stores in Tallahassee. Our grand opening was around September and the weather was still nice. With tons of sandals and wedges, we were locked and loaded.

To our surprise, the customers filled the store but they were not in search of what we had to offer. In Alabama, they were requesting boots. We could not sell them boots with $15,000 of inventory in sandals and open toe shoes. In Florida girls wear open toe shoes year round. Not knowing the market and assuming that the lay of the land was the same as it had been in Florida demonstrated a learning curve that we had not considered. We were forced to quickly make an additional investment to update our inventory.

With an updated inventory and perspective, business began to pick up. The trend that appeared to be progressing positively eventually grew somewhat stagnant. Another misconception about the prospective customers was that all of the ladies dressed up for class and to go to the club on a consistent basis. This audience was who we counted on and our most fierce level of supporters in Florida; however, this was not the case in Alabama. The mall also began to trend in a downward spiral. When we first opened the store it appeared to have been booming; however, as the months rolled by, the traffic grew less.

Not only were we not making the same money in Alabama that we had been accustomed to making in Florida, but there were also no activities for leisure that were appealing to us. The nightlife in Montgomery appealed to neither of us. It was lonely and the weather was always gloomy. We found ourselves reporting to work and back to that dry-ass apartment. The stress of it all somewhat took a toll and resulted in weight gain and a sense of stagnation. We felt secluded and the amazing world of entrepreneurship that we had created for ourselves now felt like work.

By the time spring rolled around, neither of us had to say it; we knew that it was time to cut our losses. After having experienced the process of closing a store and recognizing the importance of not being emotionally attached to making a sound business decision, the move was easy.

The necessary paperwork to break the lease was completed, and we packed our inventory and returned to Tallahassee.

Although some might view this scenario as a loss, we both recognized the tremendous win in not staying longer than necessary and refraining from positioning our business for loss. It is much better to redirect efforts sooner than later. Taking this approach allowed us to break even once the books were consolidated. In our minds, no losing also meant winning.

Verse II:
EVOLUTION IS NOT OPTIONAL

**If by chance you are brave enough
to let it all go, then you will have
wisdom to see what stays.**
-Tiff & Lex-

With what felt like two attempts to scale the boutique under our belts, we were significantly wiser than before. The continuous flow of success at BellaDonna kept us afloat and encouraged. Even so, we remained in a constant state of determining other ways to increase our reach. The concept of launching a website was the next move.

The next city that we considered would be in the state of Texas. At the time we were still party girls and Dallas, Texas proved to be a bomb location to kick it. Late nights and early mornings were in full affect. Texas was so big there was no way we couldn't consider at least one city in the DFW metroplex for expansion of the business.

Fearlessness allowed us to begin the process of prospecting the area. And because we were able to live rent-free with family, the risk was less and the potential for reward was far greater.

If the shit didn't work, we had no problem packing it all up and heading back to the crib. Texas was looking like a whole snack because we knew that we had the best products in the game and still had to make a killing out there.

Even though Houston was more popping than Dallas, we chose to set up shop in Dallas. We decided to embark upon a temporary lease at the Parks Mall. The temporary lease would give us an opportunity to get our feet wet without engaging in a massive commitment if the arrangement didn't work out. Just as we had suspected, business was booming! The foot traffic was heavy, the women had every intent to look and feel their best, and they spent hella money. By the time the stint at the Parks Mall had come to an end, there was one lesson that was more profound than all the others. We recognized that business was up and down with the brick and mortar. And even though the work we had done in Texas was fruitful, it was now more apparent than ever that we needed to establish our presence on the world wide web.

Verse III:
SEASONS CHANGE

Fight like hell for your legacy.
-Tiff & Lex-

After once believing that scaling the boutique with the exact same business plan that had been used to create the magic that materialized in the state of Florida, reality hit that our business model was not a one size fits all. The truth was that not only did every individual city have its own rules of engagement, but also every respective suburb or precinct of every city. From the diverse populations to the socio-economic status of the people who resided in a given area, and even the variation in the tastes of what styles and fashion were popular in a given demographic had to be considered. Prior to this juncture in the business, we recognized the need for a way to monetize the company and our merchandise on the world wide web, but now we were pressed. Not once did we envision BellaDonna being the only stream of income for the business. And although unspoken, we both knew that growing the company's arms and access to income was the goal. Come hell or high water, we were determined to make it happen.

At the time, e-commerce had not yet become a way of life. Consumers were very much still flocking to stores and brick and mortar reaped the benefits of their presence. We could see the next wave of what could be offered to consumers and we wanted to secure our business accordingly. Being a pioneer in your industry is a gift and at times a curse because there is no blueprint. More importantly, when you are a visionary and God gives visions to you that others might not be able to see, it makes implementation an uphill battle.

We knew that building a website that could showcase our shoes would provide us an opportunity to reach more customers and to technically have the store open, even if we were not present and working on location. We knew that it was possible because many of our vendors began to utilize websites to showcase their selections. Upon our first attempt to get our website off the ground, we paid a group of college guys who were young, talented in the tech arena and who appeared to be ambitious. They came highly recommended in the city as many of the other businesses in our network had done business with them. Ready, willing and able to reinvest in our business to realize future gains, we paid the hefty deposit that they required to get started.

After discussing the scope of work, they appeared to know exactly what we wanted and how to get us there. As the project ensued, their levels of professionalism diminished quickly. They would schedule meetings with us and not show up, not return phone call or engage in the communication to which we had been accustomed. Over time, it appeared that they knew more about building and launching websites than about e-commerce. We ended up having to go to mediation and eventually court just to retrieve the money that we had invested with them. The relationship was so strained that even after all that transpired, they vowed to relaunch our business relationship and still never came through. In the end, over the course of several months, we were never refunded all of our money and we walked away without a website.

Determined to get the new venture off the ground, we took a chance on another contractor. After disclosing our previous experience with him, he confirmed that things would not unfold in the same manner and assured us that he had the capabilities to launch our e-commerce site. After paying him, he created the framework for the site but never managed to complete the work. Several more months of chasing him and being victimized by his empty promises and our attempts to follow up with the project's progression wore on us. After having gone through the court system to resolve the previous failure, we were well aware of the money that it would cost to return to this scenario. We also knew that the time we invested in fighting him in court, we could be leveraging to attempt again. Needless to say, he never refunded us and we never heard from him again. And while we could have made the decision to throw in the towel and be complacent with the success that BellaDonna was currently experiencing, we could not stop trying simply because two contractors had not done what they were supposed to do. Entrepreneurship is often an uphill battle, oh but honey, we had our boots on and we were ready to climb.

As much as it would be majestic to say that the third time was a charm to get our website off the ground, it was not. The launch of the site was not without a series of complicated scenarios. This time, we sought the help of a trusted family member who had just graduated from college with a degree in the field specializing in the creation of websites and computer programming.

Much like the others that we previously entrusted with the scope of the world, he was confident that he could get the job done. He even went as far as coming to Tallahassee for an extended period of time to work with us. In the end, he set us up with some complicated programming company that also did not deliver. He soon began complaining that his girlfriend back at home was tripping about him being gone and he left us high and dry with an incomplete website. Needless to say, the relationship was strained from that point forward.

Circumstances surrounding the urgency of getting the website launched were also evolving as other competitors who had a wider appeal and national reach were beginning to pop up and the evolution of the shopper was in motion. The trend was something that could be seen if you looked close enough. Our greatest fear was that the brick and mortar concept would one day fizzle and we not be prepared to ride the next wave. We knew that giving up was for suckers and that we were not. Our last ditch effort was a random referral that we received. With nothing to lose, we knew that we had everything to gain.

The shit that you are willing to accept and the approach that you take toward getting a job done hits different after you have been taken advantage of one time too many. After reaching out to the contact, we stayed on that ass like white on rice. We scheduled meetings and follow-up meetings and daily check-ins to monitor the progress along the way. We set up incremental payments to add reinforcement and conducted oversight for every aspect of the launch. Come hell or high water, we were getting that site off the ground, and eventually we did. Little did we know that it would be just in time for the next phase of retail and the introduction of a phenomenon that the world now knows as social media.

Prophecies and REVELATIONS

*S*ometimes things fall apart to perfectly fit back together. Many forget that real life is happening at the same time that entrepreneurship is unfolding. To be honest, it all has the ability to hurt like hell. The glory is in the finish, the triumph and the confidence gleaned when you realize that you did what you once thought you could not. There is something revolutionary about stretching your capacity and achieving what some will never be willing to go the distance to witness. As weak as many of the moments that we experience can make us feel, your greatest strength is in your will to win. Let no one take it away from you; it is your superpower.

Divine Intervention:
MOTIVES AND INTENTIONS

*Y*our motives and intentions as an entrepreneur will keep you focused and fixated on your goals when the circumstances are not optimal. Fully understanding how what you seek to achieve will benefit you if and when you accomplish it can be the factor that makes or breaks your success. Expanding your reach and growing your audience should always be a part of your plan. Use the space below to reflect on and examine your motivations and chart your thoughts to determine areas for growth and expansion of your ideas.

What excites you about your business?

_____

_____

What is your innovative approach to sharing the news about business?

_____

_____

If you had access to a million more people, what would you tell them about your business?

_____

_____

How do you reach new people?

_____

_____

How often do you attempt to reach new people?

_____

_____

How do you measure success?

_____

_____

How will you benefit from new customers and new levels of success?

_____

_____

An Affirmation
OF ENDURANCE

My greatest glory is revealed when I rise.

I will always finish what I deem worthy of starting.

Everything about me has been masterfully

created for a time such as this.

I will run this race.

I will declare victory.

My Reflections

My Reflections

My Reflections

My Reflections

My Reflections

IV:
THE BOOK OF
VALIDATION

**Seek validation from no one except
God. To thine own self be true.**

-Tiff & Lex-

If you thought that anything you have read up to this point in the book was crazy, prepare to have your entire wig snatched. When life gives you lemons, you can always make lemonade. On other occasions, you might find yourself needing a lemon drop martini. In this era of our lives, the devil decided to get real busy. Little did he know he would meet his match and his maker. Not only were we built to withstand the trials and tribulations of both business and real life as it unfolded, but more importantly, we were Stevie Wonder to the bullshit.

TIFF

Looking back on this era of my life, there were signs of what was to come but in many ways, I ignored them when they meant sacrificing my happiness. To say that shit hit the fan is an understatement. My relationship with D-boy was a work in progress. After finding out that I wasn't the only woman in his life I must admit that my feelings changed, even though I never let him know it. I could place all the blame on him for manipulating me, but I could no longer lie to myself because my soul knew the truth.

I also knew that I deserved to be someone's center of attention. That was a huge part of the problem. I never felt like there were others when he was with me. I can't speak for all women but I can say that a lot of us find our way into the arms of another when we feel neglected. I hadn't quite done that yet, but it was coming. Even though I was focused on finding true love and building an empire with the person that made my heart smile, even if he belonged to the streets, I could not have prepared for the shit that I would later learn about D-boy.

During the daytime hours, I worked in the store alone because I knew that I could handle the traffic that came through. In the evenings, we had employees come in to assist with the increase of customers. One day in particular stands out from the rest because I was alone but damn sure could have used some help.

Two men both dressed in khakis and button-down shirts entered the store. One was noticeably larger than the other with a wide, stout frame. The other was tall in stature but hardly intimidating. Based upon their appearance and the way that they entered the store, I immediately knew that something was off. It was obvious to me that neither were in search of shoes, not even for their wives. From their looks, not even their wives would have been the type to wear BellaDonna. One paced the aisles of the store while the other walked toward me aggressively. I wasn't afraid, I just wanted to know what the hell they wanted with our store.

"May I help you?" I said as I looked down at my acrylic nail, remembering that I needed to get it repaired. The two men made eye contact with each other and there was a pause before either said anything.

Before I could utter another word, the one who had been pacing the aisles walked over and said, "Do you know who Joseph Green is?"

I raised an eyebrow in confusion and shook my head. "No," I muttered. The truth was that I had no idea who Joseph Green was. I had never heard that name before in my life. Finally, the one who had been standing there all along held up a picture that I could not deny. FUCK. It was D-boy. I screamed inside my head but I couldn't allow myself to fold in front of them. With a straight face, I shrugged my shoulders and proclaimed, "I still don't know who that is."

"Well, we have a warrant for his arrest," the heavier one uttered. Right then and there, I knew that they were feds. The most fucked-up part of all of it was that it wasn't until that day, standing there being harrassed by them, that I learned D-boy's real name. The whole time that we had been in a relationship, purchased houses and cars together and remained down for one another, he had never disclosed his true identity.

They didn't take no for an answer. One of them blurted out, "So are you sure you have no idea who this is?"

The other chimed in. "How did you even get this store? You do know that we are going to dig deeper on this, don't you?"

Man, they fucked me up. I was trying everything not to fold and I was not planning on giving them shit on D-Boy or Joseph Green, as I now knew him to be.

Filled with rage, all I could do was convince them that I didn't know shit and that I was not going to say shit. The rest of the conversation was a blur because I was both angry and scared, but eventually they eased out of the store.

I knew that it was serious because one of his homeboys had already gone to jail and another one of his folks was on the run. Shaken, dazed, and confused, I called one of the employees who was scheduled to come in later and asked if she could come immediately. She agreed, and waiting for her to get there was torture. I didn't know if they were coming back immediately or what their next move might be. I paced the aisles of the store harder than the officer had done. When she arrived, it was like I had been given a glass of water after being in the desert for days.

"Can I use your phone for a little bit?" I asked. I grabbed the phone from her hands and ran to my car. I couldn't dial D-boy's number fast enough. He answered on the first ring and I let his ass have it. I was so torn. I was angry to discover his betrayal for a second time and I was concerned because I didn't want him to get caught by the feds.

"Why the fuck didn't you tell me your real name? Who does some shit like that? Did any of this even mean anything to you?" My voice trembled with trepidation mixed with the rage of a woman scorned. I was in tears and on edge at the same time. I didn't know what to think or where to turn. There was no one that I could even tell besides Alexis, because this needed to be handled discreetly.

He began to explain. "Come on, man. Don't do that. All this shit is real. I was trying to keep you from knowing anything that might be used against you later. If you knew who I really was, they could have come for you too. I told you I was going to protect you and I have. You ain't attached to shit that they can get to you."

I butted in. "What about the houses and the cars and all that shit that's in our names? Fuck that. We have to get rid of that shit. I can't believe this!" I hung up the phone in anger and sat in the car and cried until the tears dried up. My heart couldn't take any more and I knew that the life that I had planned with D-boy would come to an end.

LEX

There was a ribbon in the sky of love and it had my name on it. It turns out that the soul who walked through the doors of Violet Haze for casual conversation had also managed to walk through the gates to my heart. And although I wasn't looking for love, it had found me and conspired with Cupid to shoot me with his arrow. We didn't waste a lot of time with the dating game because we believed ourselves to be soulmates. Soulmates don't date, they get married, and that's exactly what we did.

The wedding was a dream come true. We returned home to Miami to commit ourselves to each other and exchange our vows in front of over two hundred family members and friends. We immediately departed after the wedding for our honeymoon in the Bahamas. Those moments were pure bliss and I took my mind off work and focused on spending quality time with my new husband.

When we returned to Florida, I dove headfirst back into making sure that we were focused on growing BellaDonna. Tiff and I decided that the opportunity presented itself once again for us to try our hand in Texas. Not even two months after being married, I told my husband that I would be leaving to open a location in Texas.

At the time, I don't think that I stopped to consider how he might feel about me leaving. All I knew was that my actions were in alignment with everything that we had discussed. The plan had always been to get multiple stores off the ground in multiple locations and that was exactly what I was doing.

When I arrived in Texas, I used the same blueprint that we had used to launch all of the previous stores. In less than thirty days, the boutique was open. I settled into my new life in Texas and made plans to get the boutique popping.

My routine became monotonous. Every morning, I woke up, grabbed breakfast, and went to the mall to pick up the cash deposit. My next move always included going to deposit the money at the bank and grabbing lunch and heading back to the mall. After the mall, it was back home and attempt to get some sleep, only to wake up and do it all over again. I was so focused on doing what I had to do so that my future would be filled with the things that I wanted to do. What I did not know was that there would be a turn of the tide in Florida that would change the way that I approached how long I would be in Texas.

I still remember like it was yesterday when my phone rang unexpectedly. I saw on the screen that it was Tiff and I was sure that she was calling to tell me about another major idea she had that we needed to implement for the store. I answered the phone as I always did. "Hey girl, what's up?"

The long pause made me slightly curious. It wasn't like her to not just blurt out whatever she had to say. I could hear her breathing on the other end of the phone heavily. "Tiff. Girl, what is going on down there?"

She returned my inquiry with tears. "Lex, this shit is hot down here. You have to stay your ass in Texas. You can't come back here for now. The motherfuckin' feds was at the store. You have to stay there until I can figure this shit out." She was talking so fast that I could hardly make out what she was saying but I heard the word "feds" loud and clear and immediately knew that something must have happened with D-boy.

Unsure of what to say or how to respond, the only words that surfaced were "Well, are you okay?"

"Yeah, I'm fine, just can't believe this shit," she replied.

Never in a million years would I have expected for the store to be hot. We had nothing to do with D-boy's street business, so I had not considered that we would be caught up in any way, but I was wrong.

When we hung up the phone, I knew that I had to stay in Texas and hold everything down until things quieted down in Florida. Imagine the thoughts that ran through my mind when

I realized that I needed to tell my new husband that I was not coming home. To add insult to injury, I could not even tell him when I might be coming home because Tiff and I had to sort everything out. On one hand, I felt bad but on the other hand I didn't because I knew that we had a business to run and that we were building an empire. He'd signed up for this life. The drive and ambition that was within me could never be compromised by anyone around me. For me, walking in purpose and doing the work that is associated with it is why I exist and I only hoped that anyone who dared to love me would understand. I was called to be an entrepreneur and that was exactly what I planned to do.

Verse I:
OPERATION 40 ACRES AND A MULE

A queen has the ability to turn pain into unprecedented power.

-Tiff & Lex-

Under no circumstances did any series of events that transpired in our personal lives ever threaten to stop the spirit of hustle that lived and thrived within us. Starting from the bottom and working our way up to the top was not just a way of life; it was in our DNA. Shit had hit the fan in Florida, but that was no reason for us to stop the cash flow. We continued to run the hell out of the boutique in Florida and opened up shop in Dallas, Texas at the Parks Mall. The grind didn't stop there. We consistently searched for ways to level up our portfolios and take the cash flow up a notch, reinvesting in our businesses every step of the way. The real estate market was on the rise with opportunity for everyday people who the system was never meant to empower. We maneuvered our way through the funding process and hit the market when it was hot.

At the time, the restrictions on attaining funding were much more lenient. Our discussions now consisted of how to split the profits from the houses that we acquired as well as filling them with tenants. The additional income from the rental properties empowered us to not even need the money from BellaDonna, which meant that we could use every dollar earned to build a bigger empire. Many entrepreneurs make the mistake of attempting to live out of the profits that they are earning and to keep the business afloat. This is why some find themselves financially strapped. Our goal became to create an income that would allow us to flourish outside of the business.

Entrepreneurship has been our greatest teacher over the years. One major lesson learned along the way was that anything worth having would be accompanied with its own set of challenges. The real estate industry was no different. After the tenants whose parents paid the rent for the duration of their time in college completed their educational experience, the time came for them to move out. That meant that we were now in search of new tenants to assume the property.

The new tenant that we approved was a lady who had accepted a corporate role. For the first year, everything went in accordance with the plan. She paid her rent on time and like clockwork, we paid the money toward the mortgage and paid ourselves from any remaining earnings. She even went as far as to have us to arrange a lease purchase agreement as she felt that this could be a home that she would want to purchase.

After the second year passed, the tenant's payments began to fall behind. We were at a loss, as we had never experienced the strain of paying the mortgage in the absence of the rent paid by the tenant. We later learned that she lost her job, which explained her late payments, which eventually turned to no payment at all. And although it was not her intent to place us in a financially compromising bind, the fact of the matter was that she did.

Prior to the hardship, she had agreed to do a lease-to-purchase option. This meant that we entered into an agreement with her believing that the relationship would not only be long-term but also that it would result in her ultimately purchasing the property. Against our emotional desires, we were forced to move forward with the eviction process to accommodate the business needs that were at hand-the mortgage payments. During that process, she was able to scrape up half of the rent, but it did not assist us in covering the entire mortgage that we were responsible for paying. We had a relationship with her and we didn't want to see her fail, so we accepted the partial payment. In court, they later advised us that because of the fact that we accepted the partial payment, there would be further delay in our ability to process eviction filings. The court systems were not in our favor and it was hard to comprehend the rationale.

In our minds, the scenario was cut and dry. We had a tenant who had not paid rent and we wanted said tenant to move out of the property so that we would be positioned to place a new tenant and cover the costs of our rental property. The limbo also meant that we didn't have the excess money to cover the costs of some of the upkeep. The rental property had now become financially taxing, all due to the tenant who now abused the grace and privilege that had been awarded by the courts. By the time the courts finally came around and forced her to vacate, the property was in shambles. The home being disheveled was also an indication of the additional financial responsibility that was mounting, as we would need to invest an exorbitant amount of money just to get the place back in order.

As with any investment, there is an opportunity to win big or lose significantly. We would not end our long-term love affair with the real estate game, but the experience with the neglectful tenant taught us some very valuable lessons that we would use to level up in years to come.

Verse II:
ACTS OF GOD

When you walk in obedience of your calling, you won't have to chase opportunity; it will be attracted to you.
-Tiff & Lex-

The old adage that everything is bigger in Texas became our reality, before we knew it but not for the most obvious reasons.

Shortly after opening the store in Texas, the devastating wrath of Hurricane Katrina made its presence felt. The damage was catastrophic and many New Orleans natives found themselves displaced in Texas. And as horrific as the storm had been, there were so many families who found themselves starting from scratch to rebuild their lives. In addition to securing a place to live and food, the next most important basic need was clothing.

Having the convenience of a mall location meant that we were set up to receive the sudden influx of displaced New Orleans ladies in immediate need of new clothes and shoes. The US government did what it could could to offer resources to those in need by way of FEMA checks. Our store was suddenly flooded with new customers who had nothing except the clothes on their backs. Their stories were heart-wrenching. Retail therapy became exactly what the doctor ordered. The ladies were buying every shoe that we had in stock and in multiple colors and styles. From the outside looking in, it appeared that the regulations for how the money could be spent were either very lenient or non-existent. The store's traffic continued to grow because they had found a good thing and they told everybody. We were in awe at the way in which word of mouth evolved as one of our most prevalent sales funnels in Dallas. It was a valuable lesson on the importance of offering what customers need, which also means that they will return for more and brag about their experience.

We would never plan to benefit from the misfortune of others. We simply learned that God has the power to use random acts of trial and tribulation to position you to prosper. For us, that positioning meant following his lead to launch the Texas store and to not give up on plans for expansion simply because it had not worked in other locations. Our company was recession proof and we managed to realize a dream of expansion and be of service to those who needed us most simultaneously. Texas proved to be a place of prosperity that we would soon revisit.

Verse III:
KNOW YOUR ANGLES

Forever MOOD: CEO,OOO,OOO
-Tiff & Lex-

*C*reating a variety of income sources for our business became an intricate part of our strategy for success. We cannot stress enough the importance of entrepreneurs keeping their eyes and ears open to the potential for new streams and the development thereof. In every instance, we used what we had available to us to create more opportunity, utilize our resources at a greater capacity and to reach new audiences. The ambiance that our boutiques became known for made each location more of a hangout than a shoe store. Between the music and the caliber of people that graced our threshold, it was lit!

With the exercise of a little creativity and a lot of word of mouth, we managed to transform our Tallahassee, Florida location into a one-stop shop during the homecoming season. Riding the waves of the past homecoming seasons, we knew that we could expect large concentrations of crowds in the mall as well as in our store. What we had not yet thought of was the fact that most of the ladies who came into the store would also be in search of tickets to the most anticipated homecoming concert, which had grown in popularity.

Now in high demand, we found ourselves connecting with one of the most popular local promoters to give his ticket sales a physical location. Prior to us connecting with him, many students were forced to stand in long lines at the campus ticket office, the only place where tickets could be purchased. This was an inconvenient stop that no one ever felt like making. Our location was convenient because everyone wanted to go to the mall or needed to come to get their outfit for the clubs.

For the next five years, BellaDonna became the prime ticket outlet for concert & party goers. The promoter was selling like crazy and he was able to double his earnings with us. During that season, we were selling more tickets than shoes. From an entrepreneurial standpoint, we assessed our own surcharge so that we were paid for every ticket that we sold. Over the years, we became the exclusive retailer outlet for the tickets. We stopped having to pay for radio ads because the artists and promoters as well as the radio stations had a vested interest in selling the concerts out. The store's name was in heavy rotation on all of the local stations.

That advertisement also meant that we were growing in notoriety. The stations were literally on the radio telling folks to come to our store. During homecoming season, the additional traffic was not without challenge. The extra traffic and crowds was a great deal to manage and we found ourselves needing more manpower each year, but we made it work.

Prophecies and
REVELATIONS

othing about the way that we approached our sales funnel was traditional in the sense that we did not limit our acquisition of new business. We leveraged word of mouth, flyers, event promotions, the real estate industry and even hardship to create revenue streams. We would literally go to high traffic areas and pass out flyers from hand to hand. We talked to people and told them about what we were doing. We also considered heavily the needs of our customers at all times in any given scenario. Instead of building a brand that only provided amazing products, we built a company that women saw as a friend and one who weathered the storms of life with them.

The difference in what we have constructed and what others offer is that we were in business for the long haul. Our goal has been and will continue to be to live and grow with our customers. Customer loyalty begins with those customers who trust you to do what is right for them and to look at their lifestyles and recognize their needs. You must strive to create something that your customers will love and want to return to you for over and over again.

Divine Intervention:
COIN FINDER

Use the space below to determine what other income streams might be possible to pursue in alignment with your current business venture.

Write 3 character traits about your target customer.

_____

_____

_____

List the top 3 products or services that your business currently offers your target customer.

_____

_____

_____

List the top 3 ways that your customer benefits from your services.

_____

_____

_____

List 3 additional products or services that you believe your customers need.

_____

_____

_____

List 3 additional products or services that you can offer that does not cost you additional money to execute.

_____

_____

_____

List 3 actions that you must take to deliver the new set of products or services that you believe your customers need.

_____

_____

_____

List 3 ways that delivering a new set of products or services can increase your income.

_____

_____

_____

An Affirmation of
FINANCIAL
PROSPERITY

Money will flow to me effortlessly.

I am deserving of financial abundance.

New resources will be within my realm of possibility.

V:
THE BOOK OF IDENTIFICATION

**Everything you say and do is a
representation of your brand.**
-Tiff & Lex-

The road to success does not include shortcuts. Any place worth going will require hard work, determination, grit, and passion that surpasses all understanding. Your ambition must be the force that drives you to pursue your purpose at all costs. Entrepreneurship is not for the faint of heart but the reward is worth the toil. As Nipsey Hussle once said...The Marathon Continues.

TIFF

I began to recognize that how you love yourself is also the way you teach others to love you. I felt an increasing need to be better to myself and to clear my path for any potential blessings that God had in store for me. Taking much-needed time to work on myself was exactly what I needed to set my mind, body and soul on fire. I started attending church in heavy rotation. The church that I made my church home hosted Bible Study on Wednesdays and I busted the doors wide open. I could not be sure about anyone else but I was standing in need of prayer. The church also offered a lunch prayer break and I was the first in line at those as well.

In many ways, I was desperate to stay connected to my environment but I also felt that the city of Tallahassee was taking a toll on me. It was amazing while I was enrolled in college but the monotony of attempting to adult there began to get the best of me. There was no room for expansion as an individual or as a business owner. Most students who attend school in a college town desire to leave after graduation. Staying got the best of me. I wanted to get away and start somewhere new, even though I was not certain of where God would take me next. The city owed me nothing and I had come to what I felt was the end of my chapter there. I was physically present in Tallahassee, but my mind and my heart were already in Texas.

LEX

Leaving my husband in Florida to build my business in Texas was not an easy decision. I saw it as necessary because when we got married, I was in the thick of it. Everyone who knew me also knew that I was building my empire. The thought never crossed my mind that anyone in my circle would do anything other than support the work that I had been relentlessly executing over the years. For me, BellaDonna was not a hobby; it was a way of life. Being away from my husband as a newlywed was taxing. I did all that I knew to do to love and nurture from afar. The more days that passed, the more I missed being with him and all of the time we spent together. Were we really married if we didn't have the luxury of holding one another and the simple things like laughing at each other's jokes? The time and the distance was heavy. I switched places with Tiffanie as we repositioned and postured ourselves for expansion. While back in Florida, my husband and I discussed the prospect of moving to Texas for good. The discussions included renting out the house and our plans together. It warmed my heart that I had someone who was on the same page about our future. I was even more ecstatic to know that God had sent me someone who could see the dream. It's not every day that you meet a person who can accommodate the visions that God gives only to you. Our plan was to hire a property manager who would oversee the property's upkeep and solicitation of tenants, which would also mean extra income for us.

I felt like I had it all. A supportive husband, ambition for days and a business that was growing beyond the territory that I had imagined. Life was good.

Verse I:
AND I SHALL TELL THE WORLD

Don't allow your stiletto to touch the ground unless you intend to walk boldly.
-Tiff & Lex-

Scaling the business to another location was no longer optional. We were not interested in a trial and error scenario. Our goal was expansion. There are times when you have established a brand worthy of operation on a larger scale. You cannot be weary or wait for the perfect moment. We realized over time that nothing would be faultless about the opening of another location and that taking steps forward to brand a business that would one day become a household name would not be easy. What we knew for sure was that attempting to gain recognition on another level and to build the scope of BellaDonna would not happen in a single city. Many business books and gurus say that you should work to grow organically in your own back yard or city, and then venture out. We had grown as much as we possibly could in the small city of Tallahassee; our brand was ready for more.

With the temporary space in Texas up and running, it became an obvious contender for expansion. We put our heads together once more to determine if this was the best move for us. We had been scouting a few of the malls for several years before making the actual leap of faith. The Town East Mall became our first official location in Texas. We signed the lease and we were officially open for business in another state. This time, we would take steps to create roots to establish a future with multiple stores in multiple locations. As we saw it, the brand was growing and expanding and all of our hard work and efforts were coming together for the greater good.

After assuming the lease at the mall, we quickly began to realize that the demographic was changing. Although there was consistent foot traffic, not everyone was shopping. Mall-goers were eating, socializing, and going into the sneaker stores. Our stiletto-wearing customers seemed to have all but disappeared. We later learned that there was a flea market named Big T's nearby that many who lived in the city frequented. Though we offered a higher quality selection of shoes, the customers in the area were always in search of cheaper options. Customers would say things like, "Oh, this is the black girl shoe store" and "At Big T's, they got stuff for $20." We wanted nothing to do with the comparison, as it was the total opposite of the brand that we had constructed. Not only was the mall's demographic for shoppers different, we also found the employee concerns to be different. Turnover was high and many of the staff members we hired were unreliable and inconsistent, proving to be a big headache for us. One ray of sunshine was a young lady in high school who was very mature for her age. She was always on time and took the job seriously as an opportunity to learn and grow. Entrepreneurship has many ups and downs but for us, there were no other options. We were committed to building and our strategy was to lay brick by brick. After a full year, we renewed the lease but on a three-month contingency just in case things did not go according to plan.

Verse II:
WHEN DISASTER STRIKES

God's plans are always greater.
-Tiff & Lex-

Trouble doesn't last always, but it is at times lurking and awaiting an opportunity to rear its ugly head. Between the store in Texas and the store in Florida, change was the only thing that was certain. The Florida store experienced a shift in traffic as the mall's management moved the bus stop's prominent location. This meant that the entry point for many of the mall's patrons was not near our store. The bus stop had in the past been significant because those who arrived at the mall had to pass by our store. BellaDonna was hard to pass by and not be tempted to walk in and peruse. If we got you inside, you were not leaving empty-handed because we kept the inventory lit!

No matter how amazing your inventory is, your brand has to be stronger. We were also facing the opening of other chain retail shoe stores such as Traffik and Bakers. These shoe stores were direct competition as they served the same purpose and there was some overlap in the consumer. The goal for our brand was still high end and to mirror stores like Macy's and Dillard's, but we could not ignore the impacts of the new shoe stores that took residency in the mall.

Back in Texas, we were wrestling with a never-ending battle of shifting climate in the Town East Mall and things were also unraveling in Florida. Through it all, we were only out to build the best brand that we could with the knowledge, skills and resources that we had at our disposal. And then, the unthinkable happened. The news of the death of a young member of the FAMU Marching 100 Band due to hazing spread through the city like wildfire. The headlines and unfolding of stories garnered national media attention. Like the rest of the city, we were struck in the hearts. We had walked the campus, and the Marching 100 had been the heartbeat of our college experience. Everyone in the city was saddened and a dark cloud of despair covered the sunshine. The incident meant threatening repercussions for the school as well as the band.

Traditionally, the band had been the magnet that drew so many to the school's culture. FAMU was popping because of the football games, and the football games were popping because of the band. The Marching 100 was the heartbeat and lifeline of FAMU. The sounds of the drums and the melodic play of the instruments, whether it be trap music or classical tributes, fed our souls. The very thought of one of the members losing his life while aspiring to do the one thing that glued so many students and alumni together was piercing.

From that point forward, nothing was ever the same. His last breath also meant a loss of air for the school's band and activities. That same loss would be felt throughout the entire city. As a result of everything that transpired, the band was suspended, and morale was declining rapidly. The attendance was also affected and the lack of presence for the football games was disheartening. For us, this meant that the city's population and their energy was refocused. Homecoming, which had been historical for our business, was no longer the beacon of success that it had once represented. People were not going out like they once had, and the state of the nostalgia that everyone had been vying to experience was a memory. The turbulent times of the disaster and senseless loss of life also marked a time of great loss for what once was. Our hearts ached for the families of those involved and our minds were focused on repositioning our brand to stand tall in the wake of tragedy.

Verse III:
ARE YOU NOT ENTERTAINED?

A winner will always focus on winning.
-Tiff & Lex-

After being in business for a decade, we knew that it was time to celebrate in a way that would continue to increase awareness of our brand and give back to a city that had supported us and held us down. In many instances, businesses host a party or event that gathers people together. We wanted to show ourselves to be innovators in every sense of the word. Instead of a traditional party, we opted for a fashion show that was focused on shoes. We were blessed to barter and partner with many of our fellow entrepreneurs in the city for the various aspects of the show, which allowed us to plan a grand event without breaking the bank.

Months in advance, we hosted a casting call to source the models for the show at the store. Although we didn't know it at the time, the announcement regarding the casting call also drew more traffic and attention to the store. Many of the girls who attended the casting were already well trained models, as there were several modeling troops that had been founded at both of the universities in the city. We were blessed that we didn't have to groom them.

With even more attention on the store, we pre-sold tickets to the anniversary fashion show. We also sold tickets at the door for increased revenue.

We opted for a venue named Hotel Duval, which was the most chic location in the city at the time. It was located in the heart of Tallahassee, which also gave an upscale vibe to the event.

On the day of the show, we were pleasantly surprised. We did not anticipate it being as large as it was. We had belly dancers and pole dancers, and the costumes on the models were over the top. The clothing was minimal because the focus was on the shoes. Before us, no one had hosted a fashion shoe show.

One of the major news anchors at the local TV station served as the host.

There must've been over 250 guests in attendance. As a way to give back, we shared a portion of the proceeds with an organization called Save the Tatas. Their mission was to join in the fight against breast cancer.

The show managed to revitalize our existing audiences and introduce us to new ones. The word of mouth about the success of the show spread like wildfire. Afterward, people began asking when the next show was to be hosted. New customers were coming into the store and calling consistently with inquiries. No one had attended anything like our innovative approach to a fashion show and the city was intrigued. At the culmination of our first decade in business, we yielded a profit, increased our customer base like never before, and achieved a new branding strategy that we had not yet implemented. That night taught us that God's plans are always greater than our own.

Prophecies and
REVELATIONS

*H*ave you ever heard the saying that your new life will cost you your old one? This became our truth on so many levels. Not even the word sacrifice embodies the trials and tribulations that we faced. To chase a dream that only you can see also means to compromise relationships, health, peace of mind and sometimes even personal growth. It takes work and diligence not to lose yourself in the whirlwind of it all. Knowing what you want, what message you are purposed to tell the world and what problem you are called to solve becomes the important factors for your business and ultimately your sanity.

Divine Intervention:
BACK TO BASICS

In a single sentence, tell what your brand or business does.

_____

_____

_____

Why does your brand or business do what it does?

_____

_____

_____

What is your business or brand's personality?

_____

_____

_____

An Affirmation
OF
MANIFESTATION

I will feed my purpose.

I will triumph every storm.

I was created with divine intention.

I will overcome every fear while pursuing my dreams.

I am a magnet for the manifestation of

all that I am destined to become.

My Reflections

My Reflections

_____

_____

_____

_____

_____

_____

_____

_____

_____

_____

_____

_____

_____

_____

_____

_____

My Reflections

My Reflections

My Reflections

VI:
THE BOOK OF UNORTHODOX

The goal should always be to blow your own damn mind.

-Tiff & Lex-

There is no way to be prepared for growth. No matter how hard you try, it is not possible to predict the ways that God will stretch and expand your capacity. The good news is that you were made for this. We have all been created with infinite chambers, waiting to be filled with new experiences and knowledge to help us discover lives of abundance. The goal is not to be ready; the goal is to be willing to cast your net wider and to dream bigger. There is more that life has to offer you, if only you believe.

TIFF

After what felt like the ultimate spiritual cleanse, I was ready for love. As fate would have it, Alexis introduced me to a family friend. There was a connection. He was rebuilding his life after a stint of being locked up and I was rebuilding my mindset after self-imprisonment from a relationship that no longer served me. This time around, I was not a girl in college still trying to find her way. In many ways, I had learned to love myself, and the value that I brought to a relationship was clear. And even though I knew my worth, that could never stop me from loving hard. The thing that many fail to realize about me is that I love with my whole heart. When I give my love to someone, I give with the intent that shit will last forever and a day. I don't spend time thinking about the end; I'm always thinking about creating new beginnings. I am the personification of a ride or die chick, and not just for my romantic relationships. I go hard for anyone that I truly care about. There are times when I can do so to a fault, but at the end of the day, this is who I am and have always been.

In my new relationship, things just clicked. We shared the same circle of friends and many of our hopes and dreams mirrored each other. We moved relatively fast with intentions of building a life together. It was understood that even though I had a business in Florida, Texas was looking like the next best move. For me, love didn't mean that the hustle stopped or got put on hold; it just meant that I now had someone hustling right beside me. Having someone on my team who was willing to ride with me made me feel like I was on top of the world. More hands meant that more could get done.

We purchased a home in Texas that had enough room for Alexis and her husband as well as us. The intent was that whichever couple was in town at the time would have a place to stay, but it was also large enough that both couples could reside at the same time. Over time, the trend was that I was in Texas more working to stabilize the market and Alexis was in Florida keeping the store thriving.

Being in Texas and knowing that we were solidifying a future gave me a sense of comfort. Settling into the thought of family made me feel at ease. Not long after being in Texas full time, we learned that our family would be expanding. I was pregnant and beyond thrilled about it.

Now with a baby on the way, I felt the need to solidify my grind even more. It was now my goal to ensure that not only was my financial future secured, but now also the future of my unborn child.

LEX

One of the hardest lessons that I learned was that seasons change. That lesson was accompanied by another important lesson: people change. The relationship that Tiffanie and I had cultivated for so many years would be tested by distance and the implications of our personal affairs. Tiffanie was now in Texas and doing her best to run the three brick and mortar locations, while I remained in Florida holding down our first store. I fully trusted her to execute her new and innovative ideas in the best interest of the company that we'd dreamed of and created together. There were many times that I was unsure of the direction that she was crafting. There were so many factors that became a part of the equation. She was also expecting her first child, which meant additional stress in running the stores. She expressed to me that she was running like crazy and I recognized that a likely byproduct of our lives was decreased conversations. It was almost as if a season between us and for BellaDonna was coming to an end. I began to focus my attention toward devising a strategy that would be in the best interest of my husband and me. After submitting my application for a community college back home in South Florida, I learned of my acceptance. The news of my admittance to the community college meant that BellaDonna was now my Plan B. I would now need to find someone who could run the store in Tallahassee while I relocated with my husband to attend college. Pharmacy was my intended study of choice but I would first need to complete the prerequisites. I reached out to my brother to see if he would be willing and able to run the store in our absence. He obliged and that freed me to pursue my aspirations and dreams that had not been possible while constructing a new life in Florida. My sights were set on a new career in the medical field.

Verse I:
ONWARD AND UPWARD

We are the authors of our destinies.
-Tiff & Lex-

*O*ur team was split in half, with each of us working at stores in two different states. We had to consider if we were spreading ourselves too thin or if we had made the right decision in opening the Texas location. Still believing in our ability to grow and scale the business, we consistently made room for new opportunities as they arose. Little did we know, many major moments were on the horizon. We were still in contact with the management of all the locations that we scouted in Texas. The Parks Mall had an opening and we were elated. The location had a demographic that we knew would love our shoes and it was positioned central to nearby businesses.

After several months, we were elated to learn that our original vision would now come to fruition at Parks Mall. We set up shop quickly and got to work. Shortly thereafter, we were offered an opportunity to open a third location across the city. We were taking no prisoners and eating goals for dinner. We now had a total of three locations in Texas and one in Florida to run. Momentum was growing but so was the work associated with keeping everything afloat. One of our stores was outperforming all of the others. That location was keeping the entire franchise alive. During that era, the importance of having multiple streams of income was reinforced.

We eventually had to make the tough decision to close two stores in Texas. The dynamics of the store that was keeping us afloat was also changing. We were on a temporary lease agreement, which meant that the mall's management had the liberty to relocate us at any time. The mall shifted us around to three different locations on the same floor. In addition to all of the shifting, the rent was increasing. The hits from having to incur the cost of relocation, inclusive of new signage, and potentially decor to fill the space was burdensome. We were being drained financially, so much so that one more request for relocation would have sent us into a cash drought. In retrospect, we could no longer afford to maintain our business in that location. Our ability to launch another stream of revenue was dire.

Due to the nature of the swiftly dying market in Florida, we began considering the tough prospect of closing the store after eleven amazing years. The choice was not made in the absence of emotional hardship, but we both knew that it would potentially be best. After all, we were not going out of business; we were considering restructuring. Although a hard lesson, every business must understand when the time is right to pull the trigger to make changes before continuing to sail on a sinking ship.

These are the hard decisions associated with entrepreneurship and we were not afraid to make them, nor were we afraid to revamp a business model that we knew still had the potential to yield major dividends. Now, more than ever, we harnessed our energy toward the launch of our website. As we saw it, failure only existed when we didn't take action toward manifesting our dreams and goals. We wanted no part of that. We were in it to win it.

Verse II:
THE WORLD IS YOURS

When you unleash both inspiration and drive, abundance is the result.
-Tiff & Lex-

*T*he brick and mortar business model in Texas was taxing. As with the oversight of any retail space, the market adjusts inconsistently. This means that business owners have to find a way to sync with the ebbs and flows of a fickle industry. Always working to predict seasons of drought before they happened, we made a decision to establish the preliminary stages of building a team on the ground in Texas. This was a marketing strategy that we had not executed previously. What we knew for sure was that our ability to leverage an e-commerce model was the only place left to place our faith. The problem was that getting the website off the ground had been difficult. We were in need of the perfect person to bring it all to life.

During this same era, a budding friendship with a Queen named Trise morphed into her becoming a trusted confidant. There were countless moments and exchanges in the store, and time spent creating. Trise shared her love for fashion and operating in the creative realm. Conversations about her being in the educational system and the desire to transition into work that revolved around her purpose was constant. Trise was a Jane of All Trades. Her talents were evident when she was given the freedom to create. In the store, we would spend time spiking heels, painting on shoes and basking in her mean design skills. She had no reason to be there at the store, and her presence was a clear indicator of the type of friend she became. Trise was an all-around good person and the relationships deepened from the exchange of good energy. Not only had she become a friend in the store, but her presence was felt at events outside of the store. From moments with family to many of life's significant milestones, there were not many special times that she was not there. Her ability to create flyers and manipulate websites was also pretty dope. The fact that we were in search of someone to assist us in getting the website off the ground further proved that Trise was heaven sent. And even with all of her talents in tow, she never wanted anything in return.

The synergistic energy was evident when she visited the store. Through continued conversation it became apparent that she very much wanted to transition from her role in education to execute her vision for all things fashion and creativity. With the mounting financial implications from the store's leaking faucet of finances, we were desperately in need of someone to create looks to be featured on the website. There were now countless examples of e-commerce sites popping up. In many ways, we felt behind the gun that we had not managed to get our site live prior, but we also knew that whatever we launched needed to be aesthetically impactful and pop so that buyers would want it whether they were on the site or in the store. Driven by sheer ambition, we gave Trise the opportunity to quit her job to become our full-time creative director, and she accepted. It was a job that she had always dreamed of and exactly what we needed to shape the visuals that the brand would become known for producing. It was a match made in heaven. The amount of faith that she placed in our ability to create our vision spoke volumes about her character.

After what felt like an uphill battle, the website was finally live. We had spent so much time trying to arrive at the best name for the site. At the time, all of the stores that we admired had simple names. Bakers, Macy's, and Dillard's. BellaDonna was a little bit long, and didn't always roll off the tongue. We explored every variation of BellaDonna that we could think of. Donna B's, BELLA DONNAS SHOES and then magically, Bdonnas was unearthed. When we said it, it rolled right off the tongue. We didn't know it at the time, but we had just managed to secure the name of a branding machine that would withstand the test of time. Simply having the site up and running was only half the battle. Learning new and innovative ways to showcase the products would usher in the next level of challenges.

The thought was that if we had a storage space to house and ship our inventory, we could pay less overhead than having a physical mall location. After visiting a small storage facility in Arlington, Texas, we learned that they offered two options that could work for us. One option was a larger space and one was a smaller, more modestly priced space. At the time, we had no online sales and no online traffic. All we had was a dream of what could be. We had no real data that could assure us of what kind of profit the website had the potential to make or what the traffic would look like. Doubt whispered that the smaller space was the safest option. Ambition whispered that the bigger space meant taking a leap of faith. We chose ambition. Not only did we leap to lease the larger storage space, but we also made the decision to leap by closing down the brick and mortar at the mall. Although it was not glamorous to shut down a retail location to open a storage space, we were not concerned with practicality. We were so innovative, and we did not allow doubt to stop us from going big or going home.

In the beginning, the site made a couple hundred dollars a day. In business, nothing is ever perfect and to elevate, you must always be willing to be in a state of progression. The learning can never cease to exist. We focused our attention on diversifying the way the business received income and marketed to our clients. Our goal became to make money online. The website was always open for business.

Verse III:
QUEENS ADJUST
CROWNS

**We must seek to be relentless in
the pursuit of expansion.**
-Tiff & Lex-

With our team in place in Texas, we began to strategize ways to bring widespread awareness to our website and our products. We were making plans to make an investment of fifty thousand dollars to get the marketing efforts off the ground. Trise made the suggestion that we send a really hot pair of shoes to people that we believed to be highly influential on Instagram. The execution of this strategy was done so with the intent that the influencer that we selected to gift would post and share about the brand and our products on their respective social platforms.

Around the same time, social media began to take off in a major way. The power of seeing profiles of people and learning about them even though you had never met them opened the doors of opportunity for businesses like us, who were not afraid to reach out and connect. One day in particular, we came across the IG profile of a NYC entrepreneur/socialite @itsrichgirls. With a name like that, she had to be dope. We made the decision to message her via social media to share the news about gifting her with a pair of shoes. At the time, we had no idea if she would respond or not. To our surprise, she replied, introducing herself as Nessa, and agreed.

The process of building a connection was easier than we had imagined. Nessa was popping on social media and everyone was sending her gifts in hopes that she would share them with her fans and followers, so much so that she maintained a P.O. box just for that purpose. Somewhere along the way, she made a comment about how people would harass her to post after they sent her items. We made a mental note of that and listed it as what not to do as we forged a relationship with her. We picked out a bad pair of leopard print pumps to send. They were so hot! At least a month passed by after we sent the shoes and there was no movement or mention as we had hoped. And then it happened.

On a Friday night, seemingly out of the blue, the manifestation of a moment that can never be forgotten was real. Our messages started blowing up and people were frantically trying to reach us by phone. The mayhem that was unfolding on our Instagram account was almost unbelievable. Nessa had indeed posted a photo of the shoes and by the time we saw it on social media, it had already garnered over fifty thousand likes.

Not only did the picture go viral but it went on to become one of her most liked photos. The next flash of news took us by surprise. The website crashed. There we were long after business hours, contacting our web designer in hopes of him getting the site back up and running. He was baffled by all of the traffic that had come through the site and caused it to crash. That night he rescued us and got the site back running. Hours later, it crashed again from the influx of traffic. We were stressed but for good reason. In an attempt to establish a strategy, we posted a phone number on social media that would allow new customers to contact the store directly to place orders. Luckily, we had some employees who agreed to work later in the evening, and they were available to attend to the phones. The next move was to contact the distributor in the middle of the night to get more of the shoes. It was like nothing we had seen before. In one weekend, we went from a little under two hundred followers to over twenty thousand.

On that Friday night, one of the most profound marketing lessons that we could have ever learned was solidified. One reputable person endorsed the brand and from that point forward, we received worldwide attention. We will always pay homage to Nessa for her willingness to share her platform. From that point forward, we made a commitment to keep her laced with anything that she wanted from Bdonnas. She had earned our gratitude forever.

She had explained in a prior conversation how many times she had put people on and they turned around and sold the item that she had become known for, jewelry. We resolved that as long as we were in business, we would never sell jewelry as a sign of respect for the business that she had sent to us. In business, there are subliminal codes that call for the honor and respect of those who are not selfish with their time, talent, or treasure, Nessa was worth us vowing to respect the code. The moment that most business owners wait a lifetime for happened to us. We were officially on. The moment marked the culmination of our decade and a half of endless toil, unprecedented strategy and every ounce of blood, sweat and tears that we had within. We had arrived and it felt so good to witness the fruits of our labor.

Prophecies and
REVELATIONS

*A*s entrepreneurs, we must never forget that marketing is not a one size fits all concept. The true spirit of marketing our businesses is rooted in our ability to be individuals and to speak directly to the consumers that we have deemed to be our target audience. The most important thing that we can do is to help our customers find their voice and to feel empowered by the brands that we create.

It is imperative that we study a variety of marketing examples and then determine the best methods to get that message to the masses.

Far too often, we fail to realize that there are many powerful marketing tools within our reach. We were fearless in the development of our marketing efforts and we recognized early on in our business that if a particular strategy did not work or proved to be ineffective, adjustments needed to be made. We wanted to be innovators in our space and stopped at nothing until we created an empire that was not only buzzworthy, but one that our customers could be proud to represent and to buy from.

Divine Intervention:
A PIECE OF THE PIE

The areas listed below are critical to the marketing success of your business or brand. Use the space below to rate each factor on a scale of 1-10 with 10 being the highest rating.

Brand Awareness _____

Customer Acquisition/Retention/Loyalty/ Engagement _____

Lead Generation/Management _____

Sales _____

Website Traffic _____

An Affirmation
OF PURPOSE

My work is purposeful.

I will recognize my contributions to the world as valuable.

I will aspire to be recognized as an expert

and problem-solver in my business.

To thrive is my birthright.

To walk in abundance is my calling.

My Reflections

_____

_____

_____

_____

_____

_____

_____

_____

_____

_____

_____

_____

_____

_____

_____

_____

_____

My Reflections

My Reflections

My Reflections

My Reflections

VII.
THE BOOK OF GODSPEED

There are times when things fall apart so that only God can put them back together.
-Tiff & Lex-

Life is an anomaly in many ways. There are times when nothing makes sense and other moments that render clarity so clear that it gives way to confirmation and purpose of the events unfolding around us. No matter what happens, we must resolve to keep going and to push past every hurdle and trial, knowing that everything is working for our greater good. Faith is not optional; it must be sourced on a daily basis. All the power that we will ever need is within.

TIFF

I could not believe that the previous year of my life had been so taxing. From being pregnant, often alone, and running multiple stores, I had been exposed to a recipe for disaster. Everything that I had experienced left me physically, emotionally, and mentally depleted. From moments climbing ladders in the store to get to inventory to driving for hours each day checking on our various locations with a growing belly, I was pouring from an empty cup. I had run myself so ragged that a routine visit with my doctor led to a call for bed rest. I was devastated because I had never not been able to do whatever needed to be done for the business. Alexis trusted me to run the Texas market as I saw fit prior to her arrival and I was in no way going to let the empire that we were building falter. There are times that your body will make you rest and this was one of them for me. What I didn't know was that my mind was also racing a thousand miles per minute. I was attempting to hold everything together financially for my household. Throughout my entire life, I had always maintained excellent credit, but my focus was now set on helping my fiancé (at the time) reestablish himself as a businessman. If anyone knew what it meant to have a dream that only you can see, I did, and I wanted to do all that I could to help him get it off the ground. I began taking out loans and lines of credit, thinking he would flip the money. Big lines also denote big monthly repayment notes. The payment might have been about $750 per month, but the problem was that the money never flipped.

The project was to be a large-scale endeavour, which also meant large-scale risk. I was hustling, paying the bills, and trying to keep my credit intact. I also had a Benz, a big house, and multiple stores to manage. At my breaking point, I began to consider the prospect of filing for bankruptcy. My fiancé was against it and wanted me to avoid it at all costs. At first, I was ashamed because my credit had never been questionable and I had never been in a predicament that required such severe actions.

Against his advice, I sought the assistance of a lawyer and began taking classes to move forward with filing. I was desperate to get the debts off my back. My resolve was to file for Chapter 7 bankruptcy and I moved forward with conviction that it was the right thing to do.

No sooner had I filed than everything regarding my blemished finances began falling back in line. The failing finances were dead weight that was holding me down and impairing my ability to stay afloat in life and in business. Little did I know, God was preparing to reveal other areas of my life that were dead weight and needed to be dropped at all costs.

LEX

In life and in business, *normal* is what you determine it to be. I was torn between the dreams and goals that I had set in motion for the business and the need to make sure that I secured my financial future. My husband and I made the decision to relocate back to South Florida so that I could go full force with the pursuit of furthering my education. I enrolled in Broward Community College and officially started school again. I was right at home in the classroom because the acquisition of new information was second nature to me.

Consistent check-ins with my brother allowed me to feel at ease with what was happening with the store in Tallahassee. The flow of business was steady and didn't cause me concern. It was better that things were afloat because it allowed me to pursue my future in the lucrative medical field with a clear conscience.

My husband and I continued to work on our marriage and to be supportive of one another while developing our own rules of engagement. There was a source of tension and uneasiness because I learned of many of the hardships that Tiffanie was experiencing in her relationship. Her fiancé and my husband were friends. My hands were tied in so many ways because I overheard things that I should not have and I was caught between remaining loyal to my husband and my friendship with Tiffanie. She and I were not talking as much and I prayed desperately for her from afar. She was my girl and I was going to hold her down regardless. Being her support system looked different at this time than it had before.

The time seemed to fly by and before I knew it, I had managed to complete all of my pharmacy prerequisite courses. I set my sights on enrolling in pharmacy school. I liked the sound of my name with a Dr. in front of it. I applied at schools back in Tallahassee, which would allow me to get back to oversee the business and attend school simultaneously. My next move was to enroll in classes at Tallahassee Community College. I continued to plug away at my classes and was honored to have been accepted to the nursing program. My journey to become a pharmacist would finish before ever having the chance to get off to a running start.

Although things had been steady with the store in Florida when I arrived back to town, business was on the decline. Tiffanie had also discovered a new business model leveraging the warehouse space that we purchased and worked to convince me that it was the new wave of how we should do business. I had seen the numbers we were doing on the website and knew that there had to be some truth to her revelation. Our rekindled discussions led to talk of me coming back to Texas to put all of our combined efforts toward solidifying our empire leveraging the power of our online storefront. For me, there was never a question of if, only when. Just like that, my traditional path toward success sensor switched off and my entrepreneurship sensor switched on.

It was almost as if there was a supernatural force that dictated my movements. Even when I attempted to discover purpose outside of the business, I was always pulled back in. At the time I was not aware of how to call that force by name; today I recognize it as purpose.

Even in the pursuit of purpose that has your name written on it, there will be dark days. I could not have predicted what was next on the horizon for my personal life, but as for me and my business, I was gearing up for success in a major way.

Verse I:
DIGITALLY LIT

Money always looks better in the bank.
-Tiff & Lex-

*A*fter posting record numbers with the launch of our bdonnas.com website, we realized that the dream we had been chasing was real. It was not that we had not yet experienced confirmation. From the 50K weekends in our Florida store and the launch of multiple locations, we knew that we were walking in our purpose, but this time was special. There was a solid moment of clarity that made all of the rainy days worth it. Even though we were new to the digital space, we quickly adjusted and caught on to the trends. We had risen to the top of the game in our industry as trailblazers, a spot that we were not willing to compromise. We knew that no matter what happened, we had something that no one could counter, and that was our ability to select and maintain only the hottest selections that our customers got excited about. We had managed to learn our customers and their desires better than they knew themselves. We knew what looked good on them and that their hopes, dreams and desires could be fueled with fashion. Buying inventory from our vendors was so much more to us than picking out what was cute or trendy. Our approach was laser focused on empowering our clients to walk boldly in the lifestyle that they envisioned for themselves. Our online customers ranged from the college girls to 9-5 professionals to the Instagram models all turning the streets of their cities into runways. We were literally satisfying an indescribably insatiable appetite, one fly-ass pair of shoes at a time.

With the explosion of newfound popularity on social media, we were now in the thick of our first official year as an online boutique. In addition to the mall locations, our hands were full with management of every aspect of the business. Now, with the careful eye of a creative director in Trise, we directed our efforts to growing the Bdonnas brand on all platforms. Although we had no preliminary data to compare it to, the site continued to realize exponential growth. Our sales numbers increased daily. We continued to cultivate relationships with our vendors so that we could keep inventory fresh. Before we knew it, we were being contacted by many of the reality stars that we had once attempted to reach out to with no response. It's true that life is a boomerang of sorts; you can only get out of it what you put into it. This same truth applies in business.

Verse II:
HAPPY ENDINGS

**Every time they say you can't, be
sure to show them why you must.**
-Tiff & Lex-

Working to manage three mall locations that were geographically distant from each other was the ultimate test of endurance. The trend of one of the stores pulling the weight for all three continued, until it occurred to us that we needed to place more emphasis on leveraging the power of the website that was producing record numbers. We also began to consider how taxing the overhead from the brick and mortar stores was becoming. The need to be physically present at the store for seven days a week was cumbersome and at times it felt like we were circulating the money made at the three locations. In no way was our business underperforming, but there was something about the way that the website was generating sales and making money with half the time and effort that required a closer look. At our mall locations, rent was a minimum of eight thousand dollars monthly and the time, talent and treasure that was required to be present at all of the stores was never-ending.

Working in the warehouse space that we'd acquired was now the strategy that was most promising. Directing our attention toward sales and marketing tactics and scouting the best selection from our vendors was where we placed our emphasis. The profit from the sales being generated online felt like a reward for all of the tireless toil that we had invested in the mall locations over the years. It was as if God confirmed that our diligence was worth the effort. We never folded no matter how difficult the journey had been. Working in the warehouse allowed us to set our own hours and live a life that didn't revolve only around being at the stores. You could say that time was gifted back to us. We were liberated and free in a way that we had never experienced during our entire career as entrepreneurs. There were even days that we showed up to work at the warehouse in our pajamas. It was mind blowing to think that all we had to do was come in, pack orders, and answer emails.

The more abundance we witnessed in the warehouse, the less fruitful the brick and mortar stores were becoming. As bigger chain stores entered the mall, our top-performing location kept being moved around and forced us to relocate. These forced relocations were costly and began causing a decreasing cash flow. We were working like our backs were against the wall to keep the locations afloat. Had they asked us to relocate again, we would not have been able to sustain financially. Some hard decisions

would eventually have to be made regarding our business structure and the infrastructure of our business would soon require
an upgrade. A major key to our ability to sustain was the fact
that we were smart enough to bring an end to the business practices that no longer served us. It is not wise to continue utilizing
a business model that once worked if it no longer yields profit
or results. Most importantly, we trusted each other to make the
best decisions in the interest of the future of the business.

Verse III:
THOU SHALL MAKE A MILLI

Good things come to those who hustle.
-Tiff & Lex-

Some say that insanity is doing the same thing over and over again and expecting different results. We were the exception to that rule. Our routine consisted of taking action, analyzing what worked and repeating our processes over and over again until they manifested as profit. We also spent a great deal of time forging relationships with our wholesale vendors. They knew that they could count on us to place consistent orders and to create continuous business. Truth be told, we watched several vendors come and go over the years, but our hustle remained steady. Steadiness with the best vendors has been paramount to our success. The relationships forged became so meaningful that when we visited our vendors to place orders face to face, they confided that other top-selling and even global entities were requesting to see our orders. We became infamous for having the hottest shoes and making the best selections. We were trendsetters, which meant that we were also influencing what everyone else was doing. Although this was not widespread knowledge, we knew that our work had mass appeal. Things got so lit with our selections that the vendors were asking our opinions about their sample design concepts before they went to production. We had been in business just over a decade and our style was influencing the entire market.

The shoe selection game was on one hundred and so were our sales. Inspired would be the best word to describe the feelings associated with seeing sales grow daily and incrementally on the Bdonnas.com website. A little over a year prior, that was not an income source that we had in place. It was almost surreal to witness the reality of making money while we slept. By the time we reached the eighth month of our website being live, a routine review of the numbers reflected that we had posted over a million dollars in sales. In a small warehouse, with very low overhead, in our pajamas with the music turned all the way up, we hit a million dollars in sales in under a year. The gag was that with the rise of the website, all of the previous woes of working seven days per week, dealing with unreliable employees, and dividing our time between all of the locations was no longer necessary. The day that the mall management called to ask us if we wished to relocate again, we willfully declined the offer. The fact that we could decline and lose no sleep about it felt like freedom. The mall locations that we once coveted felt like a ball and chain and we were overly excited to end the rela-tionship. Our emotions were high and with an added level of success, our ambition was even higher.

Prophecies and **REVELATIONS**

Purpose is a peculiar concept. There have been countless boutique owners who have come before us and after us. Among them were business owners who put in the work but still closed their doors. There have been many with hopes and dreams that were left unfulfilled. The ugly truth is that not everyone survives entrepreneurship. The difference between us and those who are no longer in business is purpose. When you set out on a mission to embark upon your divine calling, nothing can keep you from it. Your destiny and your purpose will not escape you. For us, Bdonnas is a divine calling and we answered. When you determine to work in your purpose and you know with assurance that this is what you are supposed to be doing, everything aligns. You will meet the people that you are supposed to meet and the opportunities that God has reserved only for you will be yours. While those things manifest, your only goal is to get the job done by any means necessary. God will do the rest.

Divine Intervention:
VALUE
PROPOSITION

Knowing your product is of value to your customer base is paramount. Use the space below to list ten words that describe why customers should buy from your company instead of a competitor.

1. _____

2. _____

3. _____

4. _____

5. _____

6. _____

7. _____

8. _____

9. _____

10. _____

An Affirmation
OF CONFIRMATION

There are no limits on my abilities.

I will finish every goal given unto me.

I am fully capable of executing my dreams.

I will recognize the power of my thoughts.

My potential and power has no limits.

My Reflections

My Reflections

My Reflections

My Reflections

My Reflections

VIII.
THE BOOK OF
TRANSFORMATION

**A Woman Who Knows What She Brings
to The Table Also Knows That To Sit With
Another Woman Makes Her A Boss.**
-Tiff & Lex-

READER'S NOTE:

There are times when life hurts like hell. There is no way to prepare for the joy and pain associated with living. The only option that we have is to take it one day at a time and more importantly to remain steadfast in knowing that God will never leave nor forsake us. But on the days when the emotional bleeding causes us to lose our zest for life, we must learn to just let it flow. There is cleansing and healing in the blood of Jesus. In the words of Usher, sometimes you just have to let it burn. There is beauty for your ashes. Joy is sure to come in the morning.

TIFF

Whether I knew it or not, I would soon find out that post-partum depression is a motherfucker. Anyone that attempts to say that it does not exist is a boldfaced liar. No one can begin to describe what happens to a woman after she gives birth. Maybe no one warns you because everyone works so hard to forget the torment of your hormones fighting with each other to snap back into place. Maybe some women are embarrassed because of the thoughts they had or actions that they took in those moments. And then there is the possibility that many, like me, don't even realize that it is happening.

I was still drained from years of hard work. Lex and I were the personification of that no days off shit. Even today, I can't quite put my finger on how out of sorts I felt, but I can say for certain that shit was not right. Not only was I battling an internal struggle to find my new normal, but I was also adjusting to being a new mom. That act alone is on another level. To be fully responsible for the life of another human being is at times unbearable. On the other side of it all is pure joy to look into the eyes of the greatest gift that life renders. Eury, my firstborn son, was my new source of light and everything that I did was now for him.

He was also the reason I held on to the last bit of sanity that I had within me as another relationship began to take a turn for the worst.

There are times that as a woman, you just know that you are not the only one who is taking up space in the heart of the one for which you have vowed to be committed. I guess God no longer wanted for me to wonder or to sit idle with a racing mind, so he brought everything that I needed to see front and center. One day as I was at the house with the baby, a car pulled up to pick up my significant other. Based on the energy in the house and the slippery slope that we had been on, it was not hard for me to deduce that it was another woman. The fury began welling in my spirit almost instantly. When would it ever be acceptable for another woman to pick up your man from your house? Never, but it was happening to me. Before I knew it, I had wrapped up my baby and placed him in the truck with me. It was almost as if I blacked out because I vaguely remember getting in the truck. What I do remember was speeding down the streets of the subdivision behind them while distraught. At that moment, I was desperate to be seen, not just in the literal sense but seen such that he would remember who I had been to him and that we had created life together.

It wasn't until I looked over to realize that I had not even secured my baby in the car seat that reality kicked in. The only person who needed to see me was my baby. He was all that mattered. Had anything happened to either one of us because of the way that someone had not appreciated me, I could not have lived with myself. I stopped the truck at a nearby restaurant parking lot and watched them speed off. I no longer cared. I took my precious baby and secured him and made sure that he was happy. The look of innocence on his face was a gentle reminder that I had all that I needed to do what was best for me and my baby. We drove home and I took a hard look in the mirror. That day, I acknowledged that the woman staring back at me was crying out for help and the only person who had the power to save her was me.

I called my mother to see if she could help me for a bit with the baby and she obliged. After two weeks of soul searching, I found the girl that I had been looking for. She had managed to rediscover her worth and her peace of mind. She was now stronger than ever and ready to conquer the world, in heels with a baby on her hip. It was then that I knew that life could not break me, nor would God allow it to.

LEX

Three months after getting the storage space in Texas, we finalized our decision to close the store in Florida. That process required a great deal of work. You accumulate so much over the course of eleven years. We began to sell everything in the store, from inventory to the fixtures. Liquidation sales became the new norm. People were always inquiring and asking questions like, "Are y'all going out of business?" We never responded as though we were going out of business because we truly were not. We were adjusting to saturate a new market. A relocation to Texas would be in my near future. Whether or not my marriage could sustain the move would be the question.

I arranged a meeting with a property manager to reinvigorate the discussions about my husband and me relocating to Texas. On the day of the meeting, the property manager arrived at our home and conducted a series of surveys to analyze the home.

We stayed out of the way and allowed him to handle his business. At the close of the meeting, we all sat in the living room as the property manager began preparing the numbers and calculating how much he would charge for his services while we were away. My husband and I were on the same page, and awaiting the moment to finalize the business side of the deal. After about twenty minutes, the property manager let us know that he was ready for us to review the documents and data. He began explaining what he could offer and how his services would free us from worry about the property after we relocated.

As he was finishing his presentation, my husband, who had remained quiet the whole time, blurted out, "I think I am going to just stay." Before I knew it, the words "Say what now?" hurled through my lips. There was no warning, no preconceived agendas that I was aware of, and no damn logic as far as I could see. How had he just made a decision of this magnitude on the spot in front of a complete stranger but never shared his sentiments with me, his wife? Now ain't that a bitch? Texas had my name written all over it and it looked like I would be heading that way sooner than later, even if I had to go by myself.

I began to recognize that my husband's levels of drive, motivation, and hustle did not match mine. This proved to be problematic for many reasons as it meant stagnation for all of us if nothing changed. In many ways, I also felt as though I was losing myself in the marriage. I was carrying everyone's burdens emotionally and financially, and never taking time to access what I wanted, needed and deserved. I'm just one of those people who keeps it moving. That is what I have done for my entire life. Stopping to cry over spilled milk was never a part of my routine. I'm just not that girl. The only direction to move in my mind is forward. Anyone that is coming is coming and anyone who decided to stay will stay. I would learn that valuable lesson the hard way.

Verse I:
WALK A MILE IN MY STILETTOS

Life is too short to wear ugly shoes.
-Tiff & Lex-

*T*he scene in Texas was giving life on another level. We were receiving notoriety from Bdonnas on the ground in Texas as a byproduct of the hype that was generated nationally. The power of social media worked to our advantage and we had celebrities laced with our hottest shoes. Pictures of so many *it* girls wearing our collections were popping up everywhere. We also forged genuine personal relationships that would prove to be beneficial for business.

To take full advantage of our unique positioning and popularity, we set plans in motion to host a fashion shoe show in Dallas. This same concept had made crazy waves in Florida and it was our intent that the same would manifest here in Texas. Although we had no idea of what to expect, we knew that the concept had the potential to spread like wildfire and that was exactly what happened.

During that same era, the reality TV show *Love and Hip Hop* dropped on a major TV network. The cast members were another huge draw on social media and so many of them were wearing Bdonnas. The traffic and attention that was sent to our website surged. At the time, Angela Simmons, daughter of Hip Hop legend Rev Run Simmons, was hosting BET's top-rated TV show, *106 & Park*. The show was the epitome of hip hop culture and everyone who was anyone was either tuned in or sitting on the couch being interviewed. Angela was literally wearing our gear on one of the largest platforms for our customer base. Five days out of the week, she was on BET and our name got hella hot.

We had also built a relationship with celebrities by sending them products. We were doing more than dressing these girls. We were building working relationships and friendships. Our company has benefited in so many ways from the celebrity attention, and we were blessed because we never had to pay ambassadors who typically would charge hundreds to thousands of dollars per social media post. Success was all about the power of leveraging relationships. Anything the celebrities who marketed our company for free would need, we were on it. There were times that it was taxing, but the business that we received in turn was all worth it. When you move like that for folks, that is a game changer. Going above and beyond set us apart.

The more fashion shows we hosted, the more the audience and the buzz grew. Our fashion show became one of the most coveted events in Dallas. The men were showing up just as hard as the women. Much like our days of hosting in Florida, it was so much more than a fashion show. We created ambiance. At our shows, there were aerialists, stilt walkers, and even a pole dancer. We were totally entertaining the audience, which was the point of it all. The entertainment manifested into sales. By the time we got around to hosting our spring fashion show, we announced a casting call to solicit and select models. To our surprise, the line was wrapped around our building and stretched around the street corner.

The Pink Pumps & Paparazzi Shoe Show was now a household name in Dallas. Little did we know that the shows would prove to be another form of evolution for the brand. At each show, we were responsible for dressing the models. To ensure a cohesive look, we always worked hard to find the pieces that we knew accompanied our show-stopping shoes. Out of these actions, we realized that our client base was hungry for clothes as well as shoes.

The fashion shows coupled with social media presence meant that we were live and in effect on Instagram. The pictures with the various celebrities and from the shows all served as validation for the work that we had been doing for many years. We didn't care that the world was just finding out how dope we were; they needed to catch up.

Verse II:
AND YET WE RISE

**Every woman should dress as
if she's already famous.**
-Tiff & Lex-

*A*fter solidifying the new online business structure in Texas, there was no stopping us. We thought that what we'd managed to accomplish in Florida was amazing, but we had not yet seen the levels to which we had the potential to ascend. Our clientele now consisted of names like Draya Michelle, Nessa, Fantasia, Erica Dixon, Christina Milian, Karrueche, Dondria Nicole, Angela Simmons, Rah Ali, Juju, and the list goes on.

We continued to monitor the trends and adjust the way we did business. We were being featured in fashion blogs such as Fashion Bomb Daily. Erica Mena and Black Chyna were shown in another feature wearing really expensive shoes and a model wearing our shoes was featured right next to them. The feature was titled *A Look for Less*. Our version was cheaper, but still dope. A monsoon of sales resulted from that feature that had been plastered on Instagram. We had gotten so popular that people began to steal our pictures and they were reposting our images on social media as their own. The celebrity requests did not stop and we kept answering.

During this explosive era of social media and online sales, we were getting bombarded with customers looking for our physical locations. The temptation to put forth one last ditch effort with a brick and mortar came in the form of a call regarding availability once again in the Parks Mall. We decided to go for it now that our new followers and customers were searching for us. After all, the brick and mortar was the traditional format that we knew and we felt as though we owed it to ourselves to give it one last try. While there, Draya Michele and her then boyfriend Orlando Scandrick hosted their Dallas Cowboys Christmas giveaway. She was on the TV show *Basketball Wives* at the time and he was a huge star for the Dallas Cowboys. The line was wrapped around the corner and the buzz was good for the store. Though great for business, all of the new buzz from the event and social media was not enough to sustain the overhead of the mall's expenses. We resolved to close our final mall location and the chapter that included physical locations as our business model. If the bottom line is not right and it doesn't make sense, there should be no emotional ties to a particular way of handling affairs of entrepreneurship. We had learned to separate what we felt versus dollars and cents.

We also noticed a trend of big beautiful storefronts dying. Sometimes you have to put the ego aside. As long as the business model that you are executing has an active cash flow, then you do what it takes to keep that facet of your business running. You have to also be able to see the storm coming and project seasons of drought just as well as you do those of prosperity. The longer we remained in business, the more equipped we were to see into our financial future and make the necessary adjustments to keep our business up and running.

Verse III:
LIFESTYLES OF THE LIT AND FAMOUS

**Fashion is not what you wear,
it is who you are.**

-Tiff & Lex-

Due to the fact that business was going exceptionally well based on our website sales and social media presence, we directed our attention toward creating more content to maintain engagement. That engagement also came in the form of fashion shows, where we learned a great deal about what our audience wanted from us.

The fashion shows taught us that we were much more than just a brand for shoes. The introduction of clothes to our inventory was a no brainer. We had also dreamed of Bdonnas being a lifestyle brand and not just a brand that sold shoes. After our final departure from all ties with the malls, we purchased a showroom on Parry Avenue in Dallas, Texas. We now had space for extra inventory and adding clothing was the next best decision. We were always trying to introduce different items that we knew our customers would love. The showroom also offered a place for celebrity clients to come and shop in private. Although we had created the space for our inventory, it also became a popular space for celebrity fittings. We now had the city on lock for both shoes and fashion.

As the years rolled by, there were seasons that were more fruitful than others. During what we categorized as a dry summer, we were wracking our brains to unleash a new marketing strategy to revive sales. Everything was gridlocked. Although we had a large following on social media, there was no engagement, which was much different than the previous levels of success that we had experienced.

After unprecedented success and moments that many would deem historical, we found ourselves in a financial crisis. Neither of us wanted to speak about the deep levels of financial despair that we were sinking into, but that was the reality. No one wanted to be the first to bring up the subject of closing our business. It looked as if we were headed in that direction.

In a moment of bonding and complete transparency with a trusted friend by the name of Donna, CEO of a major fashion boutique, FLY JANE, we talked through what felt like demise. It was embarrassing. On the outside looking in, it appeared as if things were as they had always been. No one could tell that Bdonnas was amidst a financial drought. We were legit robbing Peter to pay Paul. Our conversations were consumed with confirmation of how much of our personal money we each needed to give to pay the bills for Bdonnas.

During the phone call with Donna, there was talk of ending it all. Her response was one that could never be forgotten. "How dare you say something like that? Look at who you are, look at what you did. It may be time to do something else, but don't you dare hold your head down about all that you have accomplished." Her words were piercing and pious. She later passed away and her expressions would be a gentle reminder to never give up. May she forever rest in paradise.

With a new perspective on life and finishing what we started, we put our brains together to determine how to increase the engagement from our already activated followers. We had the people, but our strategies were not encouraging them to buy. No one was commenting on the social media posts or asking if their size was available. One train of thought was to push a face to the forefront of the brand. For all of the years that we were in business, no one really knew who we were. Many of our customers believed that Bdonnas was a real woman. They would often call the store and when we would answer, they would say, "Oh my God, is this Bdonna?" We never countered their responses in any way. Bdonnas just became a household name and we allowed our clients to go with the way that made sense in their minds. What we didn't recognize is the correlation between having an actual face that the audience connects with and discovers themselves in. They now wanted natural bodies and a shopping tour guide.

Our previous strategy of using beautiful models to showcase the clothes was no longer resonating. We needed a new angle. As entrepreneurs, we must always keep in mind that just because something has worked in the past does not mean that it will work forever. Our previous campaigns resonated with our customers, but new times called for a new approach.

We were now face to face with our audience and hands on with our interactions. We had always known what they liked. Instead of showcasing ourselves as a massive company that did not have time to engage with our followers, we went right for their hearts to communicate directly with them via social media and to become their fashion best friends. Our customers and followers liked feeling a sense of a personal connection, and sales skyrocketed as a result of us being determined to innovate and paying close attention to the comments under our social media posts.

A closer look and a clear conscience allowed us to recognize that the photos that were getting engagement were of Tiffanie out and about on the town, draped in Bdonnas. People would always comment on the photos and ask where she had gotten her clothes from. We had never placed Tiffanie in front of the camera to be the face of Bdonnas, but from the look of the engagement, it was a strategy that we needed to explore further. The other consideration that became evident was that Tiffanie was not a model; she was a real woman. Women were growing tired of seeing fake bodies and photoshopped images of perfection. The masses were dying to see themselves in brands and to connect on a deeper level.

Trise suggested that we create some video content that included Tiffanie wearing the clothes. We were at the point of desperation and willing to try anything that could water the dry territory that we could not seem to escape. The initial concept was to have various stylists from the city of Dallas come over to our space and pick out various garb to dress Tiffanie. This could have worked, but we also realized that we did not have more to pay a stylist, which meant that we would be forced to rely on their mercy and we were not willing to place our future in the hands of someone else. We began to take matters into our own hands. After we were approved for a business line of credit, we immediately invested in our own video camera equipment and lighting. We also invested in renovating our showroom space and dressed it up to be a fabulous closet that every woman would adore.

Tiffanie got into makeup tutorials and began doing her own research on YouTube, which also meant that we would not have to pay a makeup artist. With no photographer and no videographer, we used the camera that we purchased and cell phones to capture footage of Tiffanie modeling Bdonnas attire. Our first night of filming, the selection was a pair of thigh-high boots. The boots appealed to women of all shapes and sizes because they could accommodate girls with thick thighs. That night, Tiffanie's full thighs went viral. In a matter of hours, we struck gold. Our website and social media was lit once again. That night we had to call our vendor because we were selling the boots like crazy. We went from no sales to selling about 100 pairs of shoes. God had answered our prayers and the tide turned suddenly. We had been in search of perfection when we discovered that the world had been in search of what God made.

Bdonna's Closet was officially born and the rest was history.

Donna's words were truer than ever before. "Look at who you are, look at what you did. It may be time to do something else, but don't you dare hold your head down about all that you have accomplished." God is indeed the supplier of all of our needs, if only we believe.

Prophecies and REVELATIONS

*E*ven when life appears to be throwing you stones, never forget to pick them up and build an empire of your heart's desire. Let nothing come between you and your dreams. God will clear your path of people, places and things that do not serve your purpose. When the storms of life arise, get still, quiet and allow the savage winds to carry seeds of evil away from you. Stay the course and work relentlessly until your time arrives to collect the harvest that is certain from the seeds that you have planted. In the end, you will win.

Divine Intervention:
INSTAGRAM FAMOUS

Planning your content for Instagram is never a bad idea. Use the space below to list ideas of content to share with your fans and followers on Instagram.

Day 1: _____

Day 2: _____

Day 3: _____

Day 4: _____

Day 5: _____

Day 6: _____

Day 7: _____

Day 8: _____

Day 9: _____

Day 10: _____

Day 11: _____

Day 12: _____

Day 13: _____

Day 14: _____

Day 15: _____

Day 16: _____

Day 17: _____

Day 18: _____

Day 19: _____

Day 20: _____

Day 21: _____

Day 22: _____

Day 23: _____

Day 24: _____

Day 25: _____

Day 26: _____

Day 27: ───────────────────────

Day 28: ───────────────────────

Day 29: ───────────────────────

Day 30: ───────────────────────

An Affirmation
OF CERTAINTY

I embrace the rhythm of the beats in my life.
I accept responsibility to create happiness in my heart.
My intuition is powerful and accurate.
I will take action to ensure that negativity
escapes me at all costs.
I believe in my dreams and will not stop
working until they become my reality.

My Reflections

My Reflections

_____

_____

_____

_____

_____

_____

_____

_____

_____

_____

_____

_____

_____

_____

_____

_____

_____

_____

My Reflections

_____

_____

_____

_____

_____

_____

_____

_____

_____

_____

_____

_____

_____

_____

_____

_____

_____

_____

My Reflections

My Reflections

IX:
THE BOOK OF REAPING

Even your thoughts are seeds that must be watered if you wish to reap a harvest.
-Tiff & Lex-

Never forget that a big business starts small. Entrepreneurship is reserved for those who don't mind living a few years like most people won't so that they can live a lifetime like most people can't. The goal of it all should be freedom and the gift of using your gifts and talents to impact the world. Entrepreneurship is the treasure that you present to the world on a continual basis. And even though there are times when life gets in the way, purpose will not escape you.

TIFF

In retrospect, the ugly truth was that I had once again found myself lost. In every other facet of my existence from maintaining good credit to remaining loyal to friends, doing good deeds in the world and taking good care of my money, I had passed the tests with flying colors. Besides dating D-boys, I had done life according to the rules. I filed my taxes and paid my bills on time. I maintained relationships with folks and kept in touch, just to check on them. Shit, I was a damn good person. Which was why for the life of me, I could not understand how love kept coming back to bite me. All I ever wanted was a dude who could match my ride or die mentality. Was that too much to ask? I believed in the power of love and I am proud to say that I was naïve enough to believe that if you loved someone, they would love you back with the same intensity of the love you gave to them. That was not my reality. I had been in a relationship that no longer served me and one that didn't have my best interest in mind. I never wanted to be anybody's baby's momma. I had never even been pregnant before, which further explains why I was devastated that my relationship was in turmoil.

When you are lost the way that I was lost, you are not yourself. Furthermore, you don't even know how to recognize who you are. You will not move the way that you would move if you were walking in the fullness of who God called you to be. It is as if you are boxed in, enslaved, trapped just for the sake of a relationship. And no matter how hard you try to beat the odds, a toxic relationship in your personal life will always leak into the other facets of your life.

I had shrunken myself to make my significant other feel important. My partnership with Alexis and the empire we built together had been suffering because I had lost my ability to communicate. And even though I was working myself into a frenzy, I had lost sight of our initial vision. It brings tears to my eyes and a lump wells up in my throat when I think about how my toxic relationship almost cost me Bdonnas. If you are not moving like you need to move, the whole ship can sink.

I never thought I had self-esteem problems but back then that is the only reasonable rationale for why I would have allowed someone to mistreat me the way that I was mistreated.

It was not until a random conversation with my mom that I learned how far off the deep end the relationship had taken me. My mom said, "You know, Tiff, you used to be a bulldog. You let him turn you into a poodle." She attributed the imminent struggle with me having relaxed my standards to a fault. When I came back to my senses in that relationship, it was my prayer that Alexis knew that I was back better than ever. I will forever honor Alexis for standing by me through thick and thin. I had spent my whole life in search of a relationship that would allow me to witness someone who was as ride or die as I was, never knowing that God sent me Alexis for that very reason. She stuck out the transitions of our business and the transitions of my personal life. Although we never discussed the hell that I went through and that she went through in detail, there was an unspoken declaration that we were business partners, but also the keepers of each other's souls.

LEX

The sheer fact that I had the experience of my husband telling me that he was declining to relocate with me and that I would be forced to go alone was disheartening. Right then and there, at that moment, while in the presence of a complete stranger whom we had enlisted to transition our home into a rental property upon our departure, he confirmed that he wasn't ready to leave Florida. The problem with him not being ready to leave was that I already had one foot in Texas. I wish that somebody had been there that day to pick my pride up off the floor. The myriad of emotions that I felt could not have been put into words. Let's just agree that a moment like that is always the beginning of the end. There was a whirlwind of disappointment, disbelief, frustration, and every negative thought imaginable fused with shock that overtook me. Just like that, my husband and I were married, but separate. This time for us marked the beginning of a very long physical separation that no marriage should ever have to endure.

After closing the Florida store, I immediately left and moved to Texas. To make the marriage work, I resolved to go back and forth between the two states. There was no question that the distance between us was not easy, but I did everything in my power to make it work. Neither of us knew what would happen next. Our lives went from happily ever after to taking it one day at a time.

Some might assume that I would have made the decision to stay with my husband in Florida when he proclaimed that he did not want to move to Texas. I could have decided to stop the pursuit of BellaDonna to pursue another career path—hell, I did have a college degree that I'd paid for and never used. My truth is that the dream is free and the hustle is sold separately. As much as I was willing to fight for my marriage, I also had every intention of pursuing the purpose that God had placed deep down inside of my soul. I had dreams and aspirations that I was not willing to compromise for anyone, including myself. The business has not been, nor will it ever be a Plan B for me.

Verse I:
WOMEN ARE FORCES OF NATURE

Behind every successful woman is a tribe filled with other successful women.

-Tiff & Lex-

*T*here is indeed an art to collaboration. Discovering relationships where women are already bosses in their own right is key. When everyone coming to the table brings value, no one ever has to feel like they are being shortchanged. We began collaborating with even more powerful women to launch other business ventures. Bellabody, a shapewear and fitness company, was our first collaborative business effort where we pooled our own money together to launch this new brand. We launched the company in partnership with then House of Tinks, owned by Catrina Brown and Carrielle Davidson. Catrina had her own retail store and we knew her to be credible. We had the pleasure of meeting her back when we first launched our store in Florida. Our third partner in the venture was Jacque M. We had the pleasure of meeting Jacque and becoming friends with her after moving to Texas. Jacque had been a hustler for years with an exclusive line of hand-crafted, custom made leather handbags that took the world by storm. In partnership for this venture, we made over a million dollars. Today, Bellabody is a multi-million dollar company, with previous representation by brand ambassadors including Fantasia and Juju.

The next collaborative effort we set our sights on was in the realm of real estate. For us, there were no limits on how or where we secured the bag. Our audience had been filled with women for decades who wanted the very best from life. We recognized that home ownership was at the helm of success and in many instances the difference between one's ability to generate wealth or not. Investing in real estate came second nature to us as we had been doing so since our college days. We linked up with Jacque M. once again to construct a program that would teach our clients how to become first-time home buyers. The program, affectionately named Girl Buy, was inclusive of a curriculum and a traveling course. We were inspiring and empowering women like never before. The message was fixated on securing the bag with Girl Buy before you bought the bag from Bdonnas. We envisioned a world where women bosses walk in abundance. It became increasingly imperative that we find creative ways to impart the knowledge that we'd acquired over the years to help other women to be successful. The sentiment of each one teaching one was now truer than ever for us and we continued to walk in that light in business.

Verse II:
OPERATION DIVERSIFICATION

The average millionaire has seven streams of income. What's your next best move?
-Tiff & Lex-

We've always maintained that retail has seasons of highs and lows. It is always in the best interest of the entrepreneur to watch those ebbs and flows and to position oneself to win in other arenas when the season appears to bear no fruit. We found ourselves in a sea of competition that had not previously existed. Websites were popping up left and right and there was a surge in popularity to become a boutique owner. Like us, many people were learning how to capitalize from the social media market and dominating the game required a different set of rules for engagement. It was as if everyone and their mommas wanted to own an online boutique. And to see so many entrepreneurs popping up was refreshing. We also knew that we needed to determine an exit strategy for our futures. Real estate was one market that would never go out of style.

We began researching the requirements to get licensed and to position ourselves to make money at a more significant level from buying and selling properties as well as serving as licensed agents. We arranged our partnership as we always had, where one partner hustled to fish for the business, and the other partner solidified the catch with the details, paperwork and necessary components to make business deals official. Before we knew it, we were leveraging the skills we had learned from our real estate investments during college as adults and constructing another empire in another lane to diversify our portfolios.

Verse III:
STRENGTH IN
NUMBERS

**One solid hustle has the power
to inspire another.**

-Tiff & Lex-

*F*ar too often, business owners forget that securing credit
also means securing credibility. We had always been advocates of leveraging the power of partnerships.

After a random Instagram post by a Cosmetics Queen that
the world of social media came to know as Supa Cent, we were
compelled to reach out to her. She had been notoriously recognized for posting major sales numbers during the holiday season.
Touted for making a million dollars in ninety minutes, she was
a certified boss. Her post was requesting to partner with other
women bosses and their businesses to saturate the market and

generate new sales. This strategy can be fruitful because you now have the opportunity to tap into the audience of whomever you partner with and vica versa. We continued with our campaigns and began to include her infamous Crayon Case in some of our ads. The relationship took flight as we cross promoted by posting each other's photos and including each other in our various marketing campaigns. There was no formal agreement in place and neither of us set terms as to what the other would get paid from such posts. There was no referral fee or specific ask. Our relationship was a sheer understanding of what could happen when two dope ass brands join forces. Women can work together and the narrative that tells us different is a lie. Both the Crayon Case and the products that we released during this era rose to realize major success and sales numbers. We were not strangers to collaboration and this effort proved yet again that there is strength in numbers.

Prophecies and
REVELATIONS

*T*he way that we moved in our business was a clear indicator of the people that we have always been. Even during our days at college, we demonstrated that we had the ability to be good stewards over our finances. The truth that no one is willing to disclose is that your business can only be as strong as your oversight of your financial affairs. Even if you only have a hundred dollars, a true entrepreneur knows what skill sets to leverage to get to the bag. A real boss recognizes that her ability to get to the bag and flip it is key to her success.

Divine Intervention: THE LAW OF ATTRACTION

It is imperative that you recognize and subscribe to the sentiment that you have the power to manifest anything that you set your mind, heart and actions toward. Use the space below to create a list of the top 5 things that you want to manifest in your life.

Manifestation

#1: _____

#2: _____

#3: _____

#4: _____

#5: _____

An Affirmation
OF VIBRATION

**Each new day is filled with
infinite possibilities.**

I will attract abundance in unexpected ways.

I will make meaningful contributions to the world.

I am worthy of love, abundance, happiness and fulfillment.

Giving and receiving is my greatest desire.

My Reflections

My Reflections

My Reflections

My Reflections

My Reflections

X: THE BOOK OF REAPING

Due season is coming.

-Tiff & Lex-

When your goal is to sow seeds of goodness, you will reap a harvest. No good deed goes unfertilized. As a human being as well as a business owner, life is about the ways in which you give unto others. How you determine to make the world a better place through the work of your hands is the true meaning of life and life more abundantly.

TIFF

For the first time in a long time, I felt like I could see the roses. My life was evolving, business was progressing and I had managed to secure every part of my sanctity that had been robbed from me. A part of coming full circle was the rekindling of relationships with friends. One friend in particular whom I had known several years prior repeatedly told me about her nephew. It was her desire for us to meet and to see if there was chemistry between us. At the time, I was living my best life, and truth be told, a love interest was not something that I was in search of. Even so, I accepted her invitation to attend a surprise birthday party for him. It was January and the start of a New Year. That night at the party, I saw him from a distance and I'm sure that he noticed me, but it was slightly awkward. I later learned that he was going through a pretty rough breakup, but somehow his ex was in attendance at the party and he was forced to smile as if everything was copacetic. He was dating someone at the time and I was happy to be free and clear from relationships that no longer served me.

Six months later, that same friend invited me to her family's cookout. It was the 4th of July and I was in chill mode, but agreed to join her. She was so excited about the prospect of him and me meeting once again. I was casually dressed and for certain not looking for a man. I had on some Jordans, sweats, no makeup and a wifebeater. That day when we met, it was almost as if we had known each other for awhile. We engaged in small talk for hours. Not once that day did he leave my presence. It was dope to kick it with someone and to have no real strings attached. As the cookout was drawing to a close, I could tell that he didn't want our time to end. Before I began to tell him that I was leaving, I heard him say, "What are you doing tonight? Let me take you and your girls out." I was cool with that. I was actually looking forward to having a good time. My son was gone for the summer, which meant a different level of freedom for me. I left the cookout and called my girls to meet up. By the time we got to the club, everybody was in a good mood and ready to have a good time. He kept that same energy in the club that he had earlier in the day, staying by my side. Even when the club ended, he still didn't want the night to end. He invited us to Waffle House for a nightcap.

The nightcap extended into the rest of the days of the summer. We spent every single day together hanging and doing whatever we wanted to do while enjoying each other's company. We were frequenting the strip clubs and TGI Friday's like crazy. There was not a single day that went by that he did not request to see me. He also called often, which I was not accustomed to. When we were not together, he wanted to hear my voice. I knew that he cared for me, not by what he said but through his actions. My feelings began to grow but I dared not allow myself to go too deep because I had my son Eury's feelings to consider.

When the summer of fun came to a close, I made preparations for Eury to return. In my heart, he would be the deciding factor as to whether or not I could keep the relationship going. If Eury did not approve of him or vibe with him, there would be no future plans. I had known that if this man was willing to take an interest in me and to show me love the way he had that he was special. I knew that I was a handful. At the time, business was popping and we had Dallas on lock. We were hanging with celebrities on a regular basis and truth be told, we were shining. That was just it: he let me shine. Most importantly, I could tell that he was so confident in who he was that me shining didn't change who he was or what we could be together.

After learning that Eury took to him and witnessing the bond that they forged, I knew that he was the one. He was tough yet gentle, cocky yet modest, and real. Real was not something that was foreign to me. I had been in search of someone who was as real as I was my whole life. Furthermore, he had made it clear that he was willing to accept the baggage of a broken heart that I had come to the relationship with. I was as hard as nails due to the previous hurt that I had endured. I was so intense, quoting my list of demands and making it crystal clear that I did not need a man, but he was not moved. He was solid and willing to kiss the wounds on my soul.

There was no way that I could deny that he was an alpha male but one that didn't have a need to beat his chest to tell the world. His demeanor was also responsible for diffusing scenarios that had the potential to escalate. We didn't butt heads because of the way that he was wired. As the days turned into months, the months turned into a year. After a year of dating, he made our relationship official by proposing on the beach in Jamaica for my birthday. I remained his fiancée for a year until I became his wife. I never knew love of this magnitude existed and over the years began to lose hope that it was for me, but my husband set my soul free. Today, he is my healer and my protector and every other person is a bleak memory of the past. My husband is my present and my future and together our legacy will withstand the test of time. My husband and our marriage is proof that happiness was for me all along. I just needed to wait on God to send me the man that he created for me, and eventually, he did.

LEX

My renewed conversations with Tiffanie allowed us to engage in a series of heart-to-heart moments that led to the candid truth there had been no forward progression in my marriage. I thought long and hard about the decision to bring an end to the marriage, because I saw no other way. Nothing was changing and we definitely weren't moving forward after we found ourselves living apart. After eleven faithful years, filing the paperwork was emotionally draining, but I knew that it was a decision for the best. This life of marriage with an absent husband had been my normal for so long that I was delusional about what a thriving union should look like. At some point, I got sick and tired of being sick and tired. The confusion of whether or not I was valued in the relationship at times led me to believe that I didn't know who I was. There were times that I was in a zombie mode and it was not a space that I enjoyed living in. The only remedy that I could see was taking control of my freedom.

A random conversation with a stranger was the trigger that made me see my then reality for what it was. While in conversation with a gentleman who was interested in me, he asked for my phone number. In explanation of why I could not give it to him, I confirmed that I was married. His reply dazed me. "Well, where is your husband?"

"He is in Florida," I replied.

His rebuttal stunned me. "Well, he should be here with you."

Damn. He was right. My husband should have been with me, but he was not, nor was I with him. It was then that I recognized that I was married, but living my life as though I was single. Moreover, I was in a marriage by myself.

The day that I fully executed the papers, I had moved beyond emotions. The sentiment of regret was absent. It hit me that he had never fought for our marriage at any point in time and he hadn't shown up to fight for it at the time of the divorce. Quite possibly, having nothing to fight about was a blessing in disguise. There were no children, no properties, and no finances to be discussed, which also meant that we could make a clean break. We had spent eleven years in a marriage that produced nothing.

Today, my heart is not empty, it is full. I am open for love and my heart is consumed with the love I have learned to give myself over time. I have always been a fan of love and I will never stop believing that it is for me. Until God sends me the love that he desires for me to have, I will resolve to live unapologetically. Today, I have no worries. I am simply doing me.

Verse I:
THE POWER OF CREDIT

**Beauty is in the eye of she
who holds the credit.**
-Tiff & Lex-

We found ourselves in another season of the business with different financial needs. Growing ever tired of fully financing our own ventures, we began to explore the concept of credit. The mentality that we had been exposed to dictated that one should never owe money and that cash was king. As a true entrepreneur, you are willing to gamble your personal cash to make your business or dream a reality, but in this season, we were looking to execute a different approach.

This summer in particular, we were making preparations to attend the Magic Trade Show. We had managed to attend annually, and it was the place where we shopped for inventory and set our intentions toward the new trends that we would introduce for the year. We were not cash heavy, but wanted to spend a significant amount of money to purchase new inventory. For the first time in our two decades of business ownership, we applied for a business loan. The gag was that we applied from a creditor whom we had done business with for many years prior. We had demonstrated through our interactions with our vendors and our monthly transactions that we had the ability to generate wealth and that we were good managers of our business credit. Our first loan was through American Express totaling a little under 100K. We had been operating with our old mindset for so long that we were surprised that we were approved for the loan and by the amount that we received. We paid the first loan off quickly and had major success at the trade show. We immediately understood how to use the money from the loan to scale the business to a magnitude that we had not yet reached.

With this new strategy, our personal money was now free and we were empowered in our business. The acquisition of multiple lines of credit taught us that we had been doing business way wrong, and even though our first years were stepping stones toward success, credit was an even better way to execute the financial needs of our business. We began to engage in financial forecasting, which allowed us to predict and prepare for the inevitable slow seasons. We were now ahead of the game. The more we showed ourselves to be trustworthy with the lines of credit, the more offers we received. Today, creditors throw money at us every day and we leverage the power of other people's money to build our dream empire.

Verse II:
FORECASTING THE FUTURE

You have the power to create the
future according to your dreams.
-Tiff & Lex-

*T*here is only one way to describe who we are and what we have been to the industry of fashion: TRENDSETTERS. We created a blueprint when there was not one to follow. We have opened doors of opportunity for ourselves that had not other- wise been opened. We've established a cult following of women who are proud of who they are and what they become when they align with our brand. Through it all, our mission has been to serve and to innovate. We set trends and create widespread campaigns that speak to the hearts of women who are often shut out of conversations about fashion based upon societal imposed norms of what it means to be beautiful. As the future unfolds, we have only plans to take our creativity and innovation to new levels.

Our future plans include designing our signature outerwear line and shoe collections. We have received many offers over the years, but at the helm of the culmination of two decades of revolution, we know that now is the time. There is a tremendous amount of blood, sweat, and tears that must go into the creation of our forthcoming collections, but this opportunity was created just for us.

Over the years, we have witnessed businesses come and go. We have watched shoe stores file for bankruptcy and those who maintain storefronts struggle to make ends meet. Our willingness to pivot and to scale our business meant that we became masters at the art of longevity. Today, we show no signs of slowing down. As Beyonce once said, "If you must take a risk, be willing to bet on yourself." The time is now for someone to turn up the heat in the shoe and fashion industry is now, and we, Bdonnas, will be the innovators who bring it to life.

Verse III:
THE LEVEL UP

**The act of acquiring knowledge
is the real glow up.**
-Tiff & Lex-

The greatest lesson that we have learned while building business was that the information and lessons gleaned are not purposed to remain with us. So many business owners hold back from sharing knowledge because they believe in some way that they will lose if others excel. We believe the contrary. That old saying "Each one teach one" is in alignment with what we believe and see for the future of Bdonnas. We worked tirelessly to create a platform that would empower, inspire and train the next generation of boutique owners. After putting our heads together, the brand Bdonnas Bosses was birthed. Within this space, we teach aspiring boutique owners the game and empower them with the tools to play and win. Our legacy and fate as innovators in the fashion and retail industry has been forever sealed, but for us, we will not realize history until we have opened the doors for many more who aspire to do the same. After two decades of learning and evolving, we're just getting started.

Prophecies and
REVELATIONS

As you can see, business is not for the faint of heart. Not everyone survives. There are no shortcuts to success. Every ounce of you will be required to realize your next levels. Along our journey, we gave all of ourselves to the process. The truth is that we will continue to do so because entrepreneurship with winning results dictates that you give your all. Go big or go home. What we know for certain is that if you have the will, God will always make a way.

Divine Intervention:
GRACE & MERCY

*A*bove everything else that manifests in life or your business, the exercise of gratitude must come first. Far too often, we take the people, places and things in our lives for granted. We also take all of the work that we have done for granted. The exercise of grace is for ourselves just as it is for others. Use the space below to exercise the practice of gratitude.

What are you most proud of?

_____

_____

_____

What makes you special?

_____

_____

_____

Who is someone that you appreciate?

_____

_____

_____

How can you exercise gratitude amidst a current challenge?

_____

_____

_____

What is your favorite emotion to feel?

_____

_____

_____

What do you love most about yourself?

_____

_____

_____

What area of your life can you work to demon-strate more gratitude?

_____

_____

_____

An Affirmation
OF GRATITUDE

I am happy about who I have become.

I honor my journey.

I pay homage to my destiny.

I am grateful for the people in my life.

I claim victory over my existence.

My heart is filled with grace.

My Reflections

My Reflections

My Reflections

My Reflections

My Reflections

Omega

And in the end, God called the Bosses of the world to seek passion, purpose and prosperity.

MAKE NO MISTAKE. THIS WORK IS A DIVINE CALLING.

For us, the decision to launch a business venture was fueled by a sentiment that could only be classified as passion. There are no other words that can describe the who, what, when, where, how or even why. The flicker of hope and the promise of what we had the potential to create ignited a fire that would later illuminate a path toward prosperity, not only for ourselves but also for those that we found synergy with. Prosperity can be defined in so many ways. Our definition of prosperity is not traditional in the sense that money is the sole measure. For us, prosperity is synonymous with freedom. We have been blessed to experience the bliss associated with freedom by walking in divine purpose.

The same freedom that we speak of has afforded and empowered us to honor our purpose. Purpose is a peculiar sentiment.

Some search for a lifetime to discover their why and reason for existence. We have been blessed to walk in the realm of those possibilities without apology or doubt. Even when there appeared to be an uphill climb before us, we never ceased to recognize that we were walking along the path that God created for us.

This work of changing lives through fashion is a divine calling. Many people have answered what they felt to be a divine calling, put in the work and closed the doors of their businesses. Many people have not survived the factors that we fought tooth and nail to overcome. Above all things, God never allowed us to fail.

When you are working on your purpose and you know that this is what you are supposed to do, everything aligns. In this space, we have been fortunate enough to meet the people that we were supposed to meet with the resources that we needed to make it all happen. It would not have been possible to do these things on our merit alone. Only God could have given us the divine appointment for such work. The journey has not been easy but even on our worst days, we can proudly proclaim that it has all been worth it.

A revered recipe of unprecedented trust, unapologetic ambition, and relentless friendship illuminated our pathways. Our deed and works was the litmus for two decades of innovation and the most pure form of hustle.

Today, we know without question that our business and our partnership is equally yoked. With a foundation for success intact, we are left to focus on the two acts that we have been called to do: changing lives and getting to the money.

We've been called to prosperity and it is our divine wish that you too will answer the call. Your destiny awaits.

Tiff & Lex

About the
AUTHORS

Women's fashion brand Bdonnas has remained in high demand by top celebrity stylists for their celebrity clients ranging from international recording artists, reality TV personalities and top models. Bdonnas has managed to successfully grow an organic social media following with close to 1 million followers combined.

Now, the two owners, Alexis Weekley & Tiffanie Mims, are stepping out from behind the brand with their how-to fashion eCommerce book, THE BOUTIQUE BIBLE, to help aspiring entrepreneurs who have the desire to start their own boutiques and build their own empires.

CPSIA information can be obtained
at www.ICGtesting.com
Printed in the USA
LVHW051829040520
654961LV00003B/780